WHO
SPEAKS
for
ISLAM?

WHO SPEAKS for ISLAM?

WHAT A BILLION MUSLIMS REALLY THINK

Based on Gallup's World Poll — the largest study of its kind

JOHN L. ESPOSITO & DALIA MOGAHED

Gallup Press
1251 Avenue of the Americas
23rd Floor
New York, NY 10020

Manufactured in the United States of America

First printing: 2007

10 9 8 7 6 5 4 3 2 1

Library of Congress Control Number: 2007942717

ISBN: 978-1-59562-017-0

To Drs. Salwa Rashad and Elsayed Mogahed,
my parents, who taught me to never give up.
— *Dalia Mogahed*

To Paul and Mary Pagliaro, pillars of support for
every generation of the Esposito family.
— *John Esposito*

Contents

Introduction: Islam's Silenced Majority

WHAT MANY SAW as an ongoing conflict between the United States and parts of the Muslim world intensified dramatically after the horrific events of 9/11. Violence has grown exponentially as Muslims and non-Muslims alike continue to be victims of global terrorism. Terrorist attacks have occurred from Morocco to Indonesia and from Madrid to London, and wars in Afghanistan and Iraq rage on. As of this writing, war and terrorism have claimed hundreds of thousands of lives since 9/11; the vast majority of victims have been civilians.

As we cope with savage actions in a world that seems ever more dangerous and out of control, we are inundated with analysis from terrorism experts and pundits who blame the religion of Islam for global terrorism. At the same time, terrorist groups such as al-Qaeda beam messages throughout the world that demonize the West as the enemy of Islam and hold it responsible for all the ills of the Muslim world.

Amid the rhetoric of hate and growing violence, manifest in both anti-Americanism in the Muslim world and in Islamophobia in the West, discrimination against, or hostility toward, Islam or Muslims has massively increased. In the aftermath of 9/11, President George W. Bush emphasized that America was waging a war against terrorism, not against Islam.[1] However, the continued acts of a terrorist minority, statements by

preachers of hate (Muslim and
Christian alike), anti-Muslim
and anti-West talk show hosts,

*Nearly one-quarter of Americans
say they would not want a
Muslim as a neighbor; less than
half believe U.S. Muslims are
loyal to the United States.*

and political commentators have inflamed emotions and distorted views.

The religion of Islam and the mainstream Muslim majority
have been conflated with the beliefs and actions of an extremist
minority. For example, a 2006 *USA Today*/Gallup poll found
that substantial minorities of Americans admit to harboring
at least some prejudice against Muslims and favoring heightened security measures for Muslims as a way to help prevent
terrorism. The same poll found 44% of Americans saying that
Muslims are too extreme in their religious beliefs. Nearly one-
quarter of Americans, 22%, say they would not want a Muslim
as a neighbor; less than half believe U.S. Muslims are loyal to
the United States.[2]

Are the negative perceptions and growing violence on all sides
only a prelude to an inevitable all-out war between the West
and 1.3 billion Muslims? The vital missing piece among the
many voices weighing in on this question is the actual views of
everyday Muslims. With all that is at stake for the West and
Muslim societies — indeed for the world's future — it is time
to democratize the debate.

Who Speaks for Islam?: What a Billion Muslims Really Think is
about this *silenced* majority. This book is the product of a mam-
moth, multiyear Gallup research study. Between 2001 and 2007,
Gallup conducted tens of thousands of hour-long, face-to-face

We surveyed a sample
representing more than 90%
of the world's 1.3 billion
Muslims, making this the largest,
most comprehensive study of
contemporary Muslims ever done.

interviews with residents of more than 35 nations that are predominantly Muslim or have substantial Muslim populations. The sample represents residents young and old, educated and illiterate, female and male, and from urban and rural settings. With the random sampling method that Gallup used, results are statistically valid within a plus or minus 3-point margin of error. In totality, we surveyed a sample representing more than 90% of the world's 1.3 billion Muslims, making this the largest, most comprehensive study of contemporary Muslims ever done.

After collecting vast amounts of data representing the views of the world's Muslims, we pored through that data for answers to the questions everyone is asking: What is the root of anti-Americanism in the Muslim world? Who are the extremists? Do Muslims desire democracy, and if so, what might it look like? What do Muslim women really want? The concept of this book is simple: With these questions in hand, we let the statistical evidence — the voices of a billion Muslims, not individual "experts" or "extremists" — dictate the answers.

Gallup's research produced a number of insights, but the most important was this: The conflict between the Muslim and Western communities is far from inevitable. It is more about policy than principles. *However*, until and unless decision makers listen directly to the people and gain an accurate understanding of this conflict, extremists on all sides will continue to gain ground.

The study revealed far more than what we could possibly cover in one book, so we chose the most significant, and at times, surprising conclusions to share with you. Here are just some of those counterintuitive discoveries:

- **Who speaks for the West?:** Muslims around the world do not see the West as monolithic. They criticize or celebrate countries based on their politics, not based on their culture or religion.

- **Dream jobs:** When asked to describe their dreams for the future, Muslims don't mention fighting in a *jihad*, but rather getting a better job.

- **Radical rejection:** Muslims and Americans are equally likely to reject attacks on civilians as morally unjustified.

- **Religious moderates:** Those who condone acts of terrorism are a minority and are no more likely to be religious than the rest of the population.

- **Admiration of the West:** What Muslims around the world say they most admire about the West is its technology and its democracy — the same two top responses given by Americans when asked the same question.

- **Critique of the West:** What Muslims around the world say they least admire about the West is its perceived moral decay and breakdown of traditional values — the same responses given by Americans when posed the same question.

- **Gender justice:** Muslim women want equal rights *and* religion in their societies.

- **R.E.S.P.E.C.T.:** Muslims around the world say that the one thing the West can do to improve relations with their societies is to moderate their views toward Muslims and respect Islam.

- **Clerics and constitutions:** The majority of those surveyed want religious leaders to have no direct role in crafting a constitution, yet favor religious law as a source of legislation.

Here is an overview of the main themes this book will cover:

Chapter 1: Who Are Muslims?

In many Westerners' minds, the horrific acts of 9/11 have cast a pall over Islam and Muslims. Yet, since 2002, Gallup Poll surveys indicate that a majority of Americans still say they know virtually nothing about the views and beliefs of people in Muslim countries.[3] Beyond the messages many Westerners get from sensational headlines and violent images, what do Muslims believe? What do they value? How can understanding Islam's basic beliefs shed light on contemporary issues?

Chapter 2: Democracy or Theocracy?

Is Islam incompatible with democracy? Why are there so few democracies in the Middle East? These decades-old questions continue to dominate foreign affairs. Do most Muslims want a theocracy or a democracy? George W. Bush's administration embraced the promotion of democracy as one of its rationales for the invasion of Iraq and for political transformation in the

Middle East. U.S. policy on democracy in the Middle East does dovetail with the sentiments of vast majorities of those surveyed who say they admire the West's political freedoms and they value and desire greater self-determination. But, if the desire for democracy is undisputed, then why hasn't the path toward democracy been smoother and faster? What do majorities of those in the Muslim world say about democracy and about the seriousness of United States' intent to promote it?

Chapter 3: What Makes a Radical?

The war against global terrorism has prompted many questions about the nature of global terrorism and the strategies to combat it: How much public support is there for terrorism? What are the primary drivers of such support? Do terrorist sympathizers hate the West and its way of life? How do political radicals differ from the mainstream moderate majority? What is the relationship between Islam and terrorism? What about *jihad* and suicide bombing?

Chapter 4: What Do Women Want?

For centuries, Muslim women have been the subject of intrigue as well as pity in the West. But Muslim women have seldom had the opportunity to speak for themselves, about themselves. What do Muslim women truly want? How do they view women's rights, religion, and the West? What is the most effective way to advocate for Muslim women's empowerment?

Chapter 5: Clash or Coexistence?

Crucial to the fight against global terrorism is an ability to move beyond presuppositions and stereotypes to form partnerships that transcend an "us" and "them" view of the world. Muslim partners, world governments, and all people are critical in this capacity. And yet, while Muslims and non-Muslims today are concerned about fanaticism and terrorism, they also feel under siege. Is the issue the West versus the Muslim world? Is there a clash of cultures? Is the issue religion, or is it politics? Is the key in the struggle against extremism and terrorism military action or a policy to win minds and hearts? What should be done?

Many of Gallup's findings challenge conventional wisdom and therefore will surprise and even anger many people. In the spirit of scientific inquiry, we encourage readers to question and challenge what they learn. As Albert Einstein said, "The important thing is not to stop questioning." He also said, "A man should look for what is, and not for what he thinks should be." We therefore offer what follows for your objective consideration. Let the data lead the discourse.

Chapter 1: **Who Are Muslims?**

WITH FEW EXCEPTIONS, when the Western media talks about Islam and Muslim culture, discussion tends to center on religious extremism and global terrorism: How many Muslims support extremism and terror? What is it about the religion of Islam and Muslims that produced extremism and terror? What can be done to counter and eliminate religious extremism and global terrorism? Is there hope for Islamic reform?

These are important questions, and they will be answered in the pages ahead. But to appreciate the complex and nuanced findings presented in this book, it is necessary to move beyond the sensational headlines and violent images that often influence perceptions of Islam to understand Muslims holistically. What do they believe? What principles does their faith call them to? What are their hopes and dreams?

It would be particularly helpful to provide answers to these questions to Americans, many of whom don't currently find much that is redeemable about Islam or Muslim society. In a December 2005 Gallup Poll of American households[4], when Americans were asked what they most admire about Muslim societies, the answer "nothing" was the most frequent response. The second most frequent response? "I don't know." Combined, these two responses represented the majority (57%) of Americans surveyed.

> *The majority of the world's Muslims live in Asia and Africa, not the Arab world.*

The World's Muslims: Does One Size Fit All?

While many people commonly speak of Islam and Muslims in broad, all-encompassing terms, there are many interpretations of Islam and many different Muslims. Muslims come from diverse nationalities, ethnic and tribal groups, and cultures; speak many languages; and practice distinct customs. The majority of the world's Muslims live in Asia and Africa, not the Arab world. Only about one in five of the world's Muslims are Arabs. The largest Muslim communities are in Indonesia, Bangladesh, Pakistan, India, and Nigeria rather than Saudi Arabia, Egypt, or Iran. And millions of Muslims live in Europe, the United States, and Canada, where they represent the second and third largest religion (second largest in Europe and Canada and third largest in the United States). Because of globalization and emigration, today the major cities where Muslims live are not only exotic-sounding places such as Cairo, Damascus, Baghdad, Mecca, Islamabad, and Kuala Lumpur, but also London, Paris, Marseilles, Brussels, New York, Detroit, and Los Angeles.

Religiously, culturally, economically, and politically, there are multiple images and realities of Islam and of Muslims.

Religiously, Muslims are Sunni (85%), who are the majority in most Muslim countries, or Shia (15%), who predominate in Iran, Iraq, and Bahrain. After the Prophet Muhammad died, Sunnis believed that the most qualified person should be selected as his successor. A minority, the followers of Ali (Shiites), said the Prophet Muhammad had designated Ali, his cousin and son-in-law, to be leader (*imam*) and that leadership should be within the family of the Prophet. In contrast to a Sunni caliph or ruler, a Shia *imam* is both a religious leader and a political leader and has special spiritual significance.

Further adding to the diversity, Shia Islam later split into three main divisions: the Zaydis; the Ismailis, whose leader today is the Harvard-educated Aga Khan; and the Ithna Ashari, who are majorities in Iran and Iraq. Like other religions, Islam also has different — and sometimes contending — theologies, law schools, and Sufi (mystic) orders. Finally, Muslims, whether Sunni or Shia, can be observant or non-observant — conservative, fundamentalist, reformist, secular, mainstream, or religious extremist.

The world's 1.3 billion Muslims live in some 57 countries with substantial or majority Muslim populations in Europe, North America, and across the world.[5] Major Muslim communities today are not only in Dakar, Khartoum, Cairo, Damascus, Riyadh, Tehran, Islamabad, and Kuala Lumpur, but also in London, Paris, Rome, Berlin, New York, and Washington, D.C. Muslims speak not only Arabic, but also Persian, Turkish, Urdu, Swahili, Bahasa Indonesia, and Chinese, as well as English, French, German, Danish, and Spanish.

Muslim women's dress, educational and professional opportunities, and participation in society vary significantly too. Women in some Muslim societies cannot drive cars and are sexually segregated, but women in many other parts of the Muslim world drive cars, ride motorcycles, and even fly planes. Some Muslim women are required by law to fully cover themselves in public, while others are prohibited from displaying the Muslim headscarf. A growing number of Muslim women are choosing to cover their heads, while others do not. In the United Arab Emirates and Iran, women make up the majority of university students. In other parts of the world, women lag behind men in even basic literacy.

Women serve in government in parliaments and cabinets and have headed governments in Turkey, Pakistan, Bangladesh, and Indonesia, while in other Muslim countries, women are struggling for the right to vote and run for office. Muslim women may wear a *sari*, pantsuit, blue jeans, dress, or skirt, just as Muslim men may wear long flowing robes, blue jeans, pullover sweaters, or three-piece business suits and may be bearded or clean-shaven.

Perhaps the most striking examples of diversity in the Muslim world are in economic and political development. Economically, the oil-rich and rapidly developing Persian Gulf states such as Qatar, United Arab Emirates, and Saudi Arabia are worlds apart from poor, struggling, underdeveloped countries such as Mali and Yemen. And politically, Islamic governments in Iran, Sudan, and the Taliban's Afghanistan stand in sharp relief with the more secular-oriented governments of Egypt, Syria, Turkey, and Indonesia.

In Turkey, Algeria, Jordan, Egypt, Kuwait, Yemen, Pakistan, and Malaysia, Islamic activists have emerged as an "alternative elite" in mainstream society. Members or former members of Islamic organizations have been elected to parliaments and served in cabinets and as prime ministers and presidents of countries such as Turkey, Kuwait, Jordan, Iraq, Lebanon,

Asked what they admire most about the Islamic world, the No. 1 response from significant percentages of populations in countries as diverse as Turkey, Saudi Arabia, and Indonesia is "people's sincere adherence to Islam."

Sudan, Iran, Egypt, Pakistan, Malaysia, and Indonesia. Islamic associations provide social services and inexpensive and efficient educational, legal, and medical services in the slums and many lower middle-class neighborhoods of Cairo, Algiers, Beirut, Mindanao, the West Bank, and Gaza.

All the while — and in stark contrast — militant groups have terrorized Muslim societies in the name of Islam; attacked New York's World Trade Center and the Pentagon in Washington, D.C.; and set off bombs in Madrid and London. They reflect a radicalism that threatens the Muslim and Western worlds.

The vast diversity of Islam and of mainstream moderate Muslims has been overshadowed and obscured by a deadly minority of political (or ideological) extremists. In a monolithic "us" and "them" world, Islam — not just Muslims who are radical — is seen as a global threat, and those who believe in an impending clash of civilizations are not only the bin Ladens of the world, but also many of us.

The Importance of Faith

So, what role does religion really play in Muslims' lives? According to Gallup Polls in 2001 and 2005-2007, of countries with substantial or predominantly Muslim populations, majorities in many countries (several in the 90% range) say that religion is an important part of their daily lives. Sizable percentages rate "having an enriched religious/spiritual life" as an aspect of life that is essential, that one cannot live without. Asked what they admire most about the Islamic world, the No. 1 response from significant percentages of populations in countries as diverse as Turkey, Saudi Arabia, and Indonesia is "people's sincere adherence to Islam."

Many regard religion as a primary marker of identity, a source of meaning and guidance, consolation and community, and essential to their progress. Majorities of both men and women in many predominantly Muslim countries want to see Islamic principles, *Sharia*, as a source of legislation. These respondents have much in common with the majority of Americans who wish to see the Bible as a source of legislation.[6] Both groups emphasize the importance of family values and are deeply concerned about issues of social morality. In fact, what respondents in the Muslim world *and* a significant number of Americans say they admire least about Western civilization is an excessive libertinism in society.

Islam is not to its adherents what it might appear to outside observers: simply a restrictive shell of rules and punishments. To many Muslims, it is a spiritual mental map that offers a sense of meaning, guidance, purpose, and hope. Vast majorities of residents in predominantly Muslim countries say their lives have an important purpose (90% of Egyptians, 91% of Saudis).

The importance of religion is reinforced by what Muslims say about their traditions and customs, which also continue to play a central role in their lives. When asked, "Are there traditions

Islam means "a strong commitment to God" and shares the same Arabic root as the word for peace, or *salaam*.

and customs that are important to you, or not?" majorities in many predominantly Muslim countries say "yes": Jordan (96%), Saudi Arabia (95%), Turkey (90%), and Egypt (87%). This contrasts sharply with percentages of those answering "yes" to the same question in the United States (54%) and especially in European countries such as the United Kingdom (36%), France (20%), and Belgium (23%).

If religion is regarded by so many Muslims as a core life value, beyond the sensational images and religious rhetoric of extremists, what is this faith that has won the devotion of so many? What does it mean to be Muslim? What principles call more than a billion people, with different languages and cultures, spread all over the world?

One God and Many Prophets: Basic Beliefs and Practices

Because faith is central to the lives of so many Muslims around the world, a basic understanding of Islam is necessary to fully grasp much of what is to follow. This section, which discusses the basic tenets of Islam, will be particularly useful to readers who are less familiar, or not familiar at all, with Islam.

Islam means "a strong commitment to God" and shares the same Arabic root as the word for peace, or *salaam*. Some Muslim theologians define Islam as *attaining peace through commitment to God's will*. This general definition is significant because Muslims regard anyone who meets these criteria at any

time in history to have been a "Muslim." And therefore, the
first Muslim was not the Prophet Muhammad, but Adam, the
first man and prophet of God. Islam asserts that all nations
were sent prophets and apostles (Quran 35:24) who all taught
the same basic message of belief in one unique God, and in this
regard, all the prophets are believed to have been "Muslims."

*We believe in God and what has been revealed to us; in what
was revealed to Abraham and Ismail, to Isaac and Jacob and
the tribes, and in what was given to Moses and Jesus and
the prophets from their Lord. We do not make a distinction
between any of them* [the prophets]. *For we submit to God.*
(Quran 3:84)

Like Jesus and Moses, the Prophet Muhammad (570 CE-632
CE) was born and taught his message in the Middle East, where
Islam quickly spread. Muslims worship the God of Abraham as
do Christians and Jews. Rather than a new religion, Muslims
believe Islam is a continuation of the Abrahamic faith tradition. Thus, just as it is widely acknowledged that the current
meaning of Judeo-Christian tradition was forged during World
War II, today there is growing recognition of the existence of
a Judeo-Christian-Islamic tradition, embracing all the children
of Abraham.

Muslims recognize the biblical prophets and God's revelation to
Moses (Torah) and Jesus (Gospels). Indeed, Musa (Moses), Isa
(Jesus), and Maryam (Mary) are common Muslim names. Jews,
Christians, and Muslims trace their biblical lineage to Abra-
ham. Muslims learn many of the same Old and New Testa-
ment stories and figures that Jews and Christians study (Adam

> *Jesus' mother, Mary, is mentioned by name more times in the Quran than in the New Testament.*

and Eve, Noah's Ark, the Ten Commandments, David and Solomon, Mary and Jesus), sometimes with differing interpretations. For example, in the Quran, Adam and Eve disobey God and eat the apple together, and this disobedience does not impose "original sin" on future generations. Also, Jesus' mother, Mary, is mentioned by name more times in the Quran than in the New Testament. The Quran describes Mary's virgin birth of Jesus, who is venerated as one of the great prophets in Islam but not considered divine.

According to the Quran, diversity in belief, cultures, and traditions is part of God's intended creation and a sign of his wisdom:

> *If God had so willed, He could surely have made you all one single community: but* [He willed it otherwise] *in order to test you by means of what He has given you. Race one another then in doing good works!* (Quran 5:48)

> *Among His signs is the creation of the Heavens and the Earth, and the diversity of your languages and colors. Surely there are signs for those who reflect.* (Quran 30:22)

> *O humankind, We have created you male and female, and made you nations and tribes for you to get to know one another. Indeed, the noblest of you in the sight of God is the one who is most deeply conscious of Him. Behold, God is all-knowing, all-aware.* (Quran 49:13)

Though no society is free of racial prejudice, Muslims today take great pride in what they regard as Islam's egalitarian ideals. For example, a Moroccan World Poll respondent says what he admires most about the Muslim world is Islam's message of racial equality. "I have a high regard for Islam's values and teachings and the non-racial attitudes of Muslim people."

The Quran emphasizes the unity of believers around a shared faith, regardless of ethnicity or tribe. What are the core Muslim beliefs that unite this diverse, worldwide population? As Christians look to Jesus and the New Testament and Jews to Moses and the Torah, Muslims regard the Prophet Muhammad and the Quran, God's messenger and message, as the final, perfect, and complete revelation. And, because of the remarkable success of the Prophet Muhammad and the early Muslim community in spreading Islam and its rule, Sunni Muslims look to an ideal portrait of "the first generation" of Muslims (called the companions of the Prophet) as their model — a common reference point by which to measure, judge, and reform society.

The Profession of Faith

There is no god but God [Allah] *and Muhammad is the messenger of God.*

To become a Muslim, a person simply makes this confession of faith (*shahada*). Repeated many times each day by those who pray regularly, it affirms the foundations of Islam: belief in the one, true God and his messenger, the Prophet Muhammad.

Associating anything else with God is idolatry, the one unforgivable sin. That is why Islamic art often does not depict God or the Prophet Muhammad, but relies heavily on calligraphy, geometric form, and arabesque design. However, the concept

> *"There is no god but God" means that nothing except God deserves to be "worshipped" — and this belief permeates every aspect of a Muslim's life.*

of the unity of God — in Arabic, *tawhid* — reaches beyond what many of the West might assume. It is the heart of Islam, the one fundamental idea from which everything else radiates, from Islam's principles to its practices. "There is no god but God" means that nothing except God deserves to be "worshipped" — not money, ambition, or ego — and this belief permeates every aspect of a Muslim's life, from prayer to the treatment of a neighbor to the conduct of business. If nothing is worthy of worship except God, then all humans are equal, as the Prophet Muhammad is reported to have said, "as teeth on a comb."

The second part of the declaration of faith, "Muhammad is the messenger of God," turns theory into a model for a way of life. Like Jesus in Christianity, the Prophet Muhammad, whom Muslims view as the final prophet of God, is the central role model for Muslims; but unlike Jesus for Christians, the Prophet Muhammad for Muslims is solely human. Muslims see him not only as the ideal political and military leader, statesman, merchant, judge, and diplomat, but also the ideal husband, father, and friend. The Prophet Muhammad is so revered that the name Muhammad, or names derived from it (Ahmad, Mahmud), is the most common Muslim name.

Muslims look to the Prophet Muhammad as the perfect human example of living. Volumes of stories about his life, *hadith*, record what the Prophet is reported to have said and done: how he dealt with friends and enemies, how he behaved with heads of state and with servants, how he treated his spouse or child, or how he conducted himself in battle. In his lifetime, throughout Muslim history, and today, the Prophet Muhammad is called the "living Quran," the embodiment in his behavior and words of God's will. Sunni Muslims take their name from *sunnah*, meaning those who follow the example of the Prophet Muhammad.

To help them translate the idea of *tawhid* into everyday life, Muslims are given tools called "pillars of Islam," which are supposed to help them turn theory into practice. After the first pillar, the *shahada*, is *salat*, or prayer.

Prayer

Prayer (*salat*) is a central and frequent practice for many of the world's Muslims. Five times each day, from the early morning hours until evening, the muezzin calls Muslims across the world to prayer. "Allahu Akbar . . . God is greater . . . Come to prayer . . ." The muezzin's call reminds Muslims that God is greater than whatever worldly activity they may be doing and to put it aside for a brief time of remembrance. While Muslims are encouraged to stop everything and pray right when they hear the call, they may pray later as well.

In some Muslim countries, shops are closed, office workers adjourn to a prayer room, and professionals and laborers simply stop what they are doing and face Mecca to worship God. In non-Muslim countries, many Muslims, from government officials and corporate lawyers to workers and shopkeepers, find a quiet, private place to pray. On Fridays at noon, Muslims go to a mosque for congregational prayer (*jum'a*). As we see in the Quran:

O you who believe! When the call to prayer is made on the day of congregation, go quickly to the remembrance of God, leaving business aside: That is best for you if only you knew! (Quran 62:9)

For those not within the sound of the muezzin, local prayer times are printed in virtually every Muslim newspaper. Travelers can find the specific prayer times for almost any location on the globe on the Internet or set their wristwatches to alert them. Hotel rooms in the Muslim world routinely include a small *Qibla* indicator, applied to the desk or nightstand, showing the direction of Mecca.

Many Westerners may be struck by the seemingly excessive frequency of Muslim prayer. "Five times a day seems like a lot," one American businessman admitted frankly at a recent workshop about doing business in Muslim countries. However, Salma, a practicing Muslim and an American management consultant explains *salat* this way:

How many times do people in our comfortable society eat? Dietitians recommend three meals and two snacks, but if you are a teenage male, it's more like five meals and ten snacks. Well, Islam views the human being as not only a physical being, but a spiritual being as well, and just as our physical dimension requires regular nourishment throughout the day, so does our spiritual dimension.

I pray my morning prayer at dawn before I go to work. I pray my noon and afternoon prayer at work in my office during my lunch break and as a ten-minute break in the afternoon. My other two prayers are in the evening when I

> *Muslims pray not only because it is a religious obligation, but also because it makes them feel closer to God.*

get home; one in the early evening and one before I go to bed — five small meals for the soul. I honestly cannot imagine keeping up with my hectic work and family life without this constant connection with God.

Gallup research found similar sentiment around the world. Muslims pray not only because it is a religious obligation, but also because it makes them feel closer to God. In a 2001 Gallup Poll, an overwhelming majority of respondents in seven predominantly Muslim countries indicated that prayer helps a great deal in soothing their personal worries. In six of these countries, more than two-thirds of respondents gave this response (Morocco: 83%; Pakistan: 79%; Kuwait: 74%; Indonesia: 69%; Lebanon: 68%; and Iran: 68%). Only in Turkey did as many as 6% (in contrast to the 53% who said prayer helps them a great deal) tell Gallup they felt that prayer does not help ease their personal worries.[7]

The interconnection of prayer with other important aspects of Muslim faith is captured in the saying: "Prayer carries us halfway to God; fasting brings us to the door of his praises; almsgiving procures for us admission."

The Fast of Ramadan

The month-long fast of Ramadan is a time for both physical discipline and spiritual reflection. Muslims abstain from food, drink, and sexual activity from dawn to dusk; spend time in religious reflection and prayer; perform good works; and distribute alms to help the less fortunate. At dusk, the fast is broken by a light meal. The month of Ramadan ends with one of the two major Islamic feasts (*Eids*), the Festival of Breaking the Fast, called *Eid al-Fitr*. The celebration resembles Christmas in its spirit of religious joyfulness, special celebrations, and gift-giving.

Almsgiving

Almsgiving (*zakat*, "purification") requires an annual contribution of 2.5% of all liquid assets, not just annual income, to the poor, sick, or suffering. This is not viewed as voluntary or charity, but as sharing wealth received from God. Social responsibility is emphasized in Islam. The Quran condemns the fatalistic argument that people are poor because God wills it and therefore should be left to their own destiny:

> *Thus, when they are told, "Give to others out of what God has provided for you as sustenance" the disbelievers say to those who believe, "Why should we feed those that God could feed if He wanted? Clearly, you are deeply misguided!"* (Quran 36:47)

At the same time, the Prophet Muhammad is reported to have said, *"The hand that gives is better than the hand that takes,"* encouraging self-reliance. (Sahih Bukhari, Volume 2, Book 24, Number 508)

Pilgrimage to Mecca

The declaration of faith (*shahada*), prayer five times a day, the fast of Ramadan, and *zakat* are four of the five pillars of

Islam — required observances that unite all Muslims. The fifth pillar is the pilgrimage (*hajj*) to the holy city of Mecca. Just as Muslims are united five times each day as they face Mecca in worship, so too each year, more than 2 million believers travel from all over the world to the city where the Prophet Muhammad was born and first received God's revelation. Men and women wearing simple coverings to symbolize purity, unity, and equality together participate in rituals that re-enact key religious events. There is no segregation. Muslims who have experienced the *hajj* describe the incredible experience of 2 million pilgrims chanting together as equals, entering into the divine presence, connecting them to something greater than themselves.

This experience had a transforming effect on the black activist Malcolm X, whose time at *hajj* resulted in his denouncing racist rhetoric and adopting a more inclusive understanding of human brotherhood. In a letter he wrote from Mecca, he notes his impression of *hajj*:

> There were tens of thousands of pilgrims, from all over the world. They were of all colors, from blue-eyed blonds to black-skinned Africans. But we were all participating in the same ritual, displaying a spirit of unity and brotherhood that my experiences in America had led me to believe never could exist between the white and non-white.[8]

At the end of the five-day *hajj*, Muslims throughout the world celebrate *Eid al-Adha*, the Festival of Sacrifice commemorating when God sent Abraham a ram as a substitute for sacrificing his son. This is a time of grand celebration as Muslim families, much like Jews and Christians in their celebrations of Hanukkah and Christmas, come together to visit and exchange gifts.

> *Jihad* is not associated or equated
> with the words "holy war"
> anywhere in the Quran.

Jihad: The Struggle for God

Jihad, which in the Quran means "to strive or struggle" to exert oneself to realize God's will, to lead a virtuous life, is sometimes referred to as the sixth pillar of Islam, but it has no such official status. *Jihad* is not associated or equated with the words "holy war" anywhere in the Quran. However, historically, Muslim rulers, with the support of religious scholars and officials, did use *jihad* to legitimate wars of imperial expansion. Early extremist groups also appealed to Islam to legitimate rebellion, assassination, and attempts to overthrow Muslim rulers.

The earliest Quranic verses dealing with the right to engage in a "defensive" *jihad*, or struggle, were revealed shortly after the *hijra* (emigration) of the Prophet Muhammad and his followers to Medina, where they fled persecution in Mecca. At a time when they were forced to fight for their lives, the Prophet is told: *"Leave is given to those who fight because they were wronged — surely God is able to help them — who were expelled from their homes wrongfully for saying, 'Our Lord is God'"* (Quran 22:39–40). The defensive nature of *jihad* is clearly emphasized in 2:190: *"And fight in the way of God with those who fight you, but aggress not: God loves not the aggressors."* At critical points throughout the years, the Prophet received revelations from God that provided guidelines for the *jihad*.

As the Muslim community grew, questions quickly emerged as to what was proper behavior during times of war. The Quran provided detailed guidelines and regulations regarding the conduct of war: who is to fight and who is exempted (Quran

48:17, 9:91), when hostilities must cease (Quran 2:192-193), and how prisoners should be treated (Quran 47:4). Most important, verses such as 2:194 emphasized that warfare and the response to violence and aggression must be proportional: *"Whoever transgresses against you, respond in kind."*

However, Quranic verses also underscore that peace, not violence and warfare, is the norm. Permission to fight the enemy is balanced by a strong mandate for making peace: *"If your enemy inclines toward peace, then you too should seek peace and put your trust in God"* (Quran 8:61) and: *"Had Allah wished, He would have made them dominate you, and so if they leave you alone and do not fight you and offer you peace, then Allah allows you no way against them"* (Quran 4:90). From the earliest times, it was forbidden in Islam to kill noncombatants as well as women and children and monks and rabbis, who were given the promise of immunity unless they took part in the fighting.

But what of those verses, sometimes referred to as the "sword verses," that call for killing unbelievers, such as: *"When the sacred months have passed, slay the idolaters wherever you find them, and take them, and confine them, and lie in wait for them at every place of ambush"* (Quran 9:5)? This is one of a number of Quranic verses that critics cite to demonstrate the inherently violent nature of Islam and its scripture. These same verses have also been selectively used (or abused) by religious extremists to develop a "theology of hate" and intolerance and to legitimize unconditional warfare against unbelievers.

During the period of expansion and conquest, many of the religious scholars (*ulama*) enjoyed royal patronage and provided a rationale for caliphs to pursue their imperial dreams and extend the boundaries of their empires. They said that the "sword verses" abrogated or overrode the earlier Quranic verses that limited *jihad* to defensive war. In fact, however, the full meaning and intent of the verse: *"When the sacred months have passed, slay the idolaters wherever you find them"* is missed or distorted when quoted in isolation. For it is followed and qualified by: *"But if they repent and fulfill their devotional obligations and pay the zakat* [the charitable tax on Muslims], *then let them go their way, for God is forgiving and kind"* (Quran 9:5). The same is true of another often-quoted verse: *"Fight those who believe not in God nor the Last Day, nor hold that forbidden which hath been forbidden by God and His Apostle, nor hold the religion of truth* [even if they are] *of the People of the Book,"* which is often cited without the line that follows: *"Until they pay the tax and agree to submit"* (Quran 9:29).[9]

Today *jihad* continues to have multiple meanings. It is used to describe the personal struggle to lead a good or virtuous life, to fulfill family responsibilities, to clean up a neighborhood, to fight drugs, or to work for social justice. *Jihad* is also used in wars of liberation and resistance as well as acts of terror. Religious extremist groups have assassinated Egyptian President Anwar Sadat in 1981; murdered innocent civilians in suicide bombings in Israel, Palestine, Iraq, and Afghanistan; carried out the 9/11 attacks; and have subsequently continued to engage in other acts of global terrorism in Muslim countries and in Europe. Many mainstream Muslim theologians have asserted that radicals who encourage a "jihad against the infidels" employ a faulty reading of the Quran, and they point to verses that teach that an all-powerful God could certainly eliminate disbelief if he wanted. Therefore it is not up to any Muslim to eliminate it for him by force:

> *If it had been God's will, they would not have practiced idolatry so. We have not made you their keeper, nor are you responsible for what they do.* (Quran 6:107)

> *We know best what the disbelievers say. You are not there to force them.* (Quran 50:45)

> *And if it distresses you that those who deny the truth turn their backs on you . . .* [remember that] *if God had so willed, He could bring them all to guidance. So do not join the ignorant.* (Quran 6:35)

The Quran portrays a self-sufficient God who is in no need of, and therefore prohibits, the use of force in gaining believers:

> *The throne of God extends over the heavens and the earth, and it does not weary Him to preserve them both. And He alone is truly the Most High and the Powerful. There is no compulsion in religion.* (Quran 2:255-256)

The multiple meanings of *jihad* were captured in a 2001 Gallup Poll in which 10,004 adults in nine predominantly Muslim countries were asked an open-ended question: "Please tell me in one word (or a very few words) what 'jihad' means to you."

In the four Arab nations polled (Lebanon, Kuwait, Jordan, and Morocco), the most frequent descriptions of *jihad* were "duty toward God," a "divine duty," or a "worship of God" — with no reference to warfare. However, in three non-Arab countries (Pakistan, Iran, and Turkey), significant minorities mentioned "sacrificing one's life for the sake of Islam/God/a just cause" or "fighting against the opponents of Islam." An outright majority mentioned these in non-Arab Indonesia.

In addition to the two broad categories of responses, personal definitions included:

- "a commitment to hard work" and "achieving one's goals in life"
- "struggling to achieve a noble cause"
- "promoting peace, harmony, or cooperation and assisting others"
- "living the principles of Islam"

The two broad meanings of *jihad*, nonviolent and violent, are contrasted in a well-known prophetic tradition that reports the Prophet Muhammad returning from battle to tell his followers, *"We return from the lesser jihad* [warfare] *to the greater jihad."* The greater *jihad* is the more difficult and more important struggle against ego, selfishness, greed, and evil.[10] However, it is important to note that for Muslims, whether *jihad* means a struggle of the soul or one of the sword, it is in both cases a just and ethical struggle. The word *jihad* has only positive connotations. This means that calling acts of terrorism *jihad* risks not only offending many Muslims, but also inadvertently handing radicals the moral advantage they so desperately desire.

Family and Culture

> *Most respondents in countries with sizable Muslim populations say they "have a lot of love in their life."*

Marriage and family life are the norm in Islam and at the center of community life. According to Gallup's poll of nine predominantly Muslim countries in 2001, the vast majority of Muslims considered being married and having children as extremely important (81% of Kuwaitis and Moroccans, for example, hold this view). This is reflected in many respondents' descriptions of their aspirations for the future, in which a significant number expressed the hope to find a "loving spouse" and start a family. Family bonds are among the aspects of Islamic societies that Muslims say they most admire, signaling that family is not only something Muslims value, but an attribute of their society they take pride in. Not surprisingly, most respondents in the 2005-2007 survey of countries that are predominantly Muslim or have sizable Muslim populations say they "have a lot of love in their life" (95% of Egyptians and 92% of Saudis, for example).

The importance of family comes into sharper focus in the status afforded to motherhood, defined by respondents in the 2001 poll of predominantly Muslim countries as "a gift of God, a source of everything in existence." Women have always been seen as the bearers of culture, the center of the family unit that provides a force for moral and social order and the means of stability for the next generation.

A famous *hadith* explains Islam's reverence for mothers: A man asked the Prophet Muhammad who was most worthy of honor, to which the Prophet responded, *"Your mother."* The man was undoubtedly surprised at this response, considering the patriarchal nature of traditional tribal societies. He went on to ask the Prophet again, "And who next?" The Prophet again responded, *"Your mother."* Bewildered, the man asked a third time, "And who next?" The Prophet again responded, *"Your mother."* Finally, in response to the fourth repetition of the question, the Prophet responded, *"Your father."* (Sahih Muslim Chapter 1, Book 32)

Family law is viewed as the "heart of the *Sharia*" and the basis for a strong, Islamically oriented family structure and society. In the 19th century, the family provided religious, cultural, and social protection from colonial and Western domination, as well as a site for political resistance. In a rapidly changing, unpredictable, and sometimes hostile 20th century, the family in many Muslim countries came to face economic, political, and personal pressures brought about by unemployment and economic need and by disruption from war and forced migration.

Debates in many parts of the Muslim world center on the changing roles and rights of men, women, and children in modernizing societies. These debates come into sharp focus as some respondents cite the breakdown of the traditional family as an aspect of the Western societies they least admire, as these verbatim survey responses from Pakistan illustrate:

> "18-year-old youngsters are independent to make any decision, and parents have no importance; they misbehave with parents."

> "They are vulgar with no respect for elders."

"They have weak family bonds and don't care for others' feelings."

Memory of a Glorious Past

Many Muslims, educated and uneducated, remember well the stories of a romanticized Islamic past that celebrates heroes and great empires. These stories, along with the message of the Quran and life example of the Prophet Muhammad, are deeply valued sources of inspiration and guidance and give the Muslim community a strong sense of identity.

Within 100 years of the Prophet Muhammad's death, Muslims created an empire extending from North Africa to the Indian subcontinent — an empire greater than Rome at its zenith. From the 7th to the 18th centuries, to be a Muslim was to live in an Islamic empire or one of many sultanates stretching from Timbuktu to Mindanao.

Muslims also produced a rich Islamic civilization, promoting religious and cultural synthesis and exchange. With significant assistance from Christian and Jewish subjects, Muslims collected the great books of science, medicine, and philosophy from the West and the East and translated them into Arabic from Greek, Latin, Persian, Coptic, Syriac, and Sanskrit.

The age of translation was followed by a period of great creativity as a new generation of educated Muslim thinkers and scientists made their own contributions to learning in philosophy, medicine, astronomy, optics, art, and architecture.

Muslims were skilled mathematicians. In fact, algebra comes from the Arabic word *al-Jabr*.

The cultural traffic pattern was again reversed when Europeans, emerging from the Dark Ages, turned to Muslim centers of learning to regain their lost heritage and to learn from Muslim advances in philosophy, mathematics, medicine, and science. Ironically, until recently, these Muslim accomplishments have not been recognized or taught in the West. Just as few recognize a Judeo-Christian-Islamic tradition, very few realize the role of Islamic civilization and Muslim contributions to the development of Western civilization.

For many Muslims, a religious worldview and memory of Islamic empires and sultanates, which were wealthy, powerful, and successful, validated Islam's message and the rewards for faithfulness to God. On the other hand, some interpret the failures and subjugation of Muslims to foreign forces during European colonialism, or what is seen as American neocolonialism today, as well as the perceived corruption of local governments, as a failure to remain faithful to God, to follow the straight path of Islam.

In an often-repeated *hadith*, the Prophet Muhammad is reported to have told a group of companions that they would know whether God is pleased with the Muslim community by looking to its leadership. If God is pleased with a community, *"He will put the best among them as their leader."* But if he is displeased, *"He will allow the worst among them to lead."* Today, as many Muslims critique their societies for political corruption, the lack of political freedom, and economic stagnation (while admiring the West for political and economic advancements), they look to Islam, not to Western values, as the way forward, with majorities in many of the surveyed countries associating progress of Muslim societies with "attachment to their moral and spiritual values."

What Are Muslim Hopes and Dreams Today?

Muslims face many of the same issues and concerns that any other people do. When asked about their hopes and dreams, many respondents first cite economic issues: better economic conditions, employment opportunities, and improved living standards for a better future. These are followed by the need to improve law and order, eliminate civil tensions and wars, and promote democratic ideals in their political systems, as well as enhancing their countries'international status and independence to earn more respect from others and stop outside interference. At the same time, domestic priorities include access to better educational systems to eradicate illiteracy and ignorance and to achieve gender equality, social justice, and religious freedom.

Religion and Politics

Many Muslims see their religion as much more than a personal faith. In contrast to the belief in separation of church and state, religion and society and faith and power are closely bound and intertwined in Islam. Throughout much of history, to be a Muslim was not simply to belong to a faith community or mosque but to live in an Islamic community/state, governed by Islamic law. Historically, Islam has significantly formed and informed politics and civilization, giving rise to vast Islamic empires and states as well as Islamic civilization.

Like people of other faiths, Muslims continue to pursue a further understanding and interpretation of their faith. The development of Islamic law, theology, and mysticism reflects this complex process.

Religious doctrines, laws, and practices do not come merely from clear prescriptions in sacred texts, but also from fallible, limited interpreters whose conclusions reflect their intelligence, political and social situations and customs, and the influences of power and privilege. For example, that interpreters and guardians of Islam were mostly males living in patriarchal societies naturally affected Islamic law and thought — especially interpretations regarding women and the family.

Like Jews and Christians, Muslims today contend with questions about how their faith relates to reason, science, and technology on a range of issues: evolution, birth control, artificial insemination, transplants, ecology, nuclear energy, and issues of war and peace. Many seek to draw on the pluralism and flexibility inherent in Islam in the modern age. They are fighting two battles: one against the extremists who claim exclusive ownership of the truth of Islam, and another against those of us who strengthen the extremists by equating this minority with the religion of Islam rather than considering it a dangerous aberration.

*Arabs make up only roughly 20%
of the global Muslim population.*

Muslims today struggle to
redefine their religious tradition within a modern, secular world.
Should Islam today be restricted to personal life or be integral
to the state, law, and society? Is Islam compatible with modern
forms of political participation such as democracy — or human
rights and the status of women and religious minorities or non-
Muslims? We will explore these questions and others in the
coming chapters.

KEY POINTS:

* The many languages, customs, and ethnicities of the Muslim
world illustrate its vast diversity. There are 57 countries around
the world that are majority Muslim or have significant Muslim
minorities — Arabs make up only roughly 20% of the global
Muslim population.

* Faith and family are core values in Muslims' lives, and Muslims
regard them as their societies' greatest assets.

* Muslims, like Christians and Jews, believe in the God of
Abraham and recognize biblical prophets such as Abraham,
Moses, and Jesus.

* *Jihad* has many meanings. It is a "struggle for God," which includes a struggle of the soul as well as the sword. The Islamic war
ethic prohibits attacking civilians.

Chapter 2: **Democracy or Theocracy?**

WHEN I WAS clearing immigration in London on the way to Edinburgh, an immigration official asked me, John, "What will you be doing in Edinburgh?" When he heard my response: "To keynote a conference on Islam and democracy," he smiled, stamped my passport, and said, "That will be a brief speech!"

His comments echoed the conviction among many in government, think tanks, and the media that Islam or Muslims are inherently incompatible with democracy. Pundits, academics, and government officials throughout Europe and the United States have reinforced this view.

In the aftermath of 9/11, Francis Fukuyama, a former neoconservative theorist, wrote:

> Modernity has a cultural basis. Liberal democracy and free markets do not work everywhere. They work best in societies with certain values whose origins may not be entirely rational. It is not an accident that modern liberal democracy emerged first in the Christian west, since the universalism of democratic rights can be seen as a secular form of Christian universalism. . . . But there does seem to be something about Islam, or at least the fundamentalist versions of Islam that have been dominant in recent

years, that make Muslim societies particularly resistant to modernity.[11]

British Prime Minister Tony Blair used the following argument to justify the invasion of Iraq:

> This new world faces a new threat: of disorder and chaos born either of brutal states like Iraq, armed with weapons of mass destruction; or of extreme terrorist groups. Both hate our way of life, our freedom, our democracy.[12]

A diverse group of government officials, members of Congress, and pundits, echoing academic experts such as Samuel Huntington and Bernard Lewis, warn of the dangers of "a clash of civilizations." This belief has deep roots among policy makers and experts and is partly in response to some of the political realities of the Muslim world:

- Only one in four Muslim majority countries have democratically elected governments.

- Rulers in a number of Muslim countries with alleged democratic elections routinely win presidential elections by roughly 90% to 99.9%. Tunisia's president, Ben Ali, won 99.4% of the vote in the 1999 presidential elections and 94.5% in 2004. In Egypt, President Hosni Mubarak won in 1999 with 94% and in 2005 with 88.6% of the vote.

- A majority of Muslim governments control or severely limit opposition to political parties and non-governmental organizations (NGOs). They have the power

> *U.S. policy on democracy in the Middle East does dovetail with the sentiments of vast majorities of those surveyed who say they admire the West's political freedoms and they value and desire greater self-determination.*

to license and ban or dissolve them, as well as to control their ability to hold public meetings and to access the media.

For example, in 2001, two years after King Abdullah of Jordan ascended the throne, he dissolved parliament at the end of its term and used "security" as a justification for delaying elections for two more years.[13] President Hosni Mubarak of Egypt suddenly canceled municipal elections scheduled for spring 2006 out of fear of the Muslim Brotherhood's growing popularity after it won one-fifth of the seats in the 2005 legislative elections.[14] Because the Muslim Brotherhood is still outlawed in Egypt, its candidates must run as independents. Although polls were conducted in Saudi Arabia in 2005 to elect town councils, the councils have little to no power. Many reforms promised by senior princes have not materialized.[15]

Against this backdrop, President George W. Bush signaled the importance of addressing the democracy deficit in the Muslim world, identifying democratization as a key goal of American foreign policy, and for good reason. Democracies are more stable than dictatorships. Stable democracies limit the conditions that breed political conflict, radicalization, violence, and terrorism.

U.S. policy on democracy in the Middle East does dovetail with the sentiments of vast majorities of those surveyed who say they admire the West's political freedoms and they value and desire greater self-determination. But, if the desire for democracy is undisputed, then why hasn't the path toward democracy been smoother and faster? Gallup World Poll data on respondents' views of democracy and U.S. foreign policy provide an important perspective on commonalities and distinctive differences in expectations, goals, and ways to get there.

While the spread of democracy has been the stated goal of the U.S. government, majorities in Jordan, Egypt, Iran, Pakistan, Turkey, and Morocco disagree that the United States is serious about spreading democracy in their region of the world.

The recent change in the Bush administration's rhetoric on democratization in the Arab world would seem to reinforce these attitudes, especially considering Secretary of State Condoleezza Rice's visit to the Middle East in January 2007. Two years earlier, when Rice canceled a scheduled visit to Egypt to protest the arrest of Ayman Nour — a leading liberal, democratic politician — Rice sent the message that the Bush administration was serious about pushing for democratic reform in the Arab world. When she did visit Egypt in early 2006, she spent most of the time discussing the need for Egypt's push for democracy and reform. However, when Rice returned to that country a year later, she reportedly made no public mention of Egypt's regression on democracy and reform. Although Nour, the Egyptian president's closest challenger in the 2005 presidential elections, was thrown in prison again and the country had rolled back on progress it made on free speech and dissent, Rice instead described Egypt's authoritarian regime as part of "an important strategic relationship, one that we value greatly."[16]

The direction of the Bush administration's new strategy in the Middle East is to reinforce the United States' historical alliances with the same autocratic Sunni Arab regimes whose repression has been blamed for fostering extremism and the likes of al-Qaeda. Rice now describes Egypt, Jordan, and the six Gulf autocrats as "responsible leaders," as they form the thrust of the anti-Iran alliance in the region.[17]

Disenchantment with U.S. policy in the region is reflected in the Arab press. Lebanese journalist Michael Young says:

> The American agenda has completely changed. What Iraq was set out to be has been supplanted by a completely different agenda — containing Iran and containing Iran's allies. . . . The democracy debate has ended today, and I regret that.[18]

In the aftermath of the 2006 Israeli-Hezbollah conflict in Lebanon and the U.S. decision to cut off funding to the Palestinian government after Hamas was elected, the Arab press has become increasingly vocal in pointing out U.S. "double standards" in its promotion of democracy. An editorial in the English-language *Syria Times* said: "Bush and his neo-conservative aides are still determined to fight the whole world using false mottos and hypocrisy. In practice, they are standing far away from the principles of freedom, independence and democracy."[19]

Writing in *Tishrin*, a Syrian newspaper, Izz-al-Din al-Darwish said:

> In Lebanon, the US Administration wants to annihilate the resistance through tampering with the Lebanese fabric and reviving a sectarian and denomination strife. It wants to

Many in the Muslim world say political freedom and liberty, and freedom of speech, is what they admire most about the West.

push the traders of politics and blood to the forefront and to apply pressure on the Arab and international levels to impose them as rulers of Lebanon.

Al-Darwish's commentary also accused the United States of meddling in Palestinian politics to ensure Fatah's victory despite voters' support for Hamas:

> In the Palestinian territories, this administration wants to stop the interaction between the leaders and the grassroots, besiege the resistance, and drive a wedge between the elected government and the people, in harmony with the Israeli occupational plans. The result was this fighting between the brothers.[20]

Yet, although many don't believe that the United States is serious about democracy in their regions, many in the Muslim world say political freedom and liberty, and freedom of speech, is what they admire most about the West. Large percentages also associate a "fair judicial system" and "citizens enjoying many liberties" with Western societies. At the same time, lack of unity, economic and political corruption, and extremism are what many respondents least admire about the Arab and Muslim world.

Democracy and Islam

Many in the Muslim world and in the West differ on the ways to reach democratic governance. Significant questions remain:

How can democracy thrive in countries with authoritarian cultures? Can democracy exist where religion and politics are intertwined? The electoral victories of Shiites in Iraq and Hamas in Palestine seem antithetical to Western democracy's separation of church and state. Is it possible to have democracy and *Sharia*?

Although many Muslim and Western governments talk about democracy, self-determination — as understood by the majority of those polled — does not require a separation of religion and state. Poll data show that large majorities of respondents in the countries surveyed cite the equal importance of Islam and democracy as essential to the quality of their lives and to the future progress of the Muslim world. Politics and Islam have been mixed from Egypt, Morocco, Turkey, and Jordan to Pakistan, Malaysia, and Indonesia, where Islamically oriented candidates and/or parties have succeeded in national and local elections.

Along with indicating strong support for Islam and democracy, poll responses also reveal widespread support for *Sharia*. Commonly thought of in the West as a harsh and primitive code of law, *Sharia* represents something very different for many Muslims. *Sharia* literally means "the path to water" but means "the path to God" when used in a religious context and symbolizes a path of both spiritual and societal guidance. *Sharia* represents the moral compass of a Muslim's personal and public life. So what are Muslims calling for when they say they want *Sharia* as a source of legislation? The answer to this is as diverse as the Muslim community.

Historically, the principles of *Sharia* could be used to limit the power of the sultan. A Muslim writer for *aljazeera* magazine,[21] Sheikha Sajida, wrote in October 2006:

> It's logical to install Sharia Law in Arab and Muslim states, where the majority of the population is Muslim. It's the only way for Muslims to escape the dictatorship and oppression of some of the Arab rulers, those who favor perceived self-interest over what's best for their nations.[22]

In response to a question posted on the "Let's Talk" section, Sajida continues:

> Islam advocates justice and I see no conflict between Islamic law and human rights. On the contrary, applying Islamic law in Muslim states safeguards human rights against the oppression of some of the Arab rulers who are only focused on how to use their influence to the utmost before they lose the throne.

When the Nigerian state of Kano first announced it would apply *Sharia* in 2000, for example, many Nigerians gathered to celebrate the decision in the state capital's main prayer grounds. Hassan Dambaba, a teacher who was present at the proclamation ceremony, said, "It is the fulfillment of our dreams. Now we can practice our religion as we should."[23]

The world's attention turned to Nigeria in 2002 when a 30-year-old Nigerian woman, Amina Lawal, was sentenced to death by stoning. In response to her pregnancy out of wedlock, the Islamic court convicted her of adultery, punishable by stoning,

> *Sharia* as a source of legislation today draws strong support from more than 7 in 10 Nigerian Muslims who say they want *Sharia* as at least a source of legislation — 1 in 5 wants it as the only source.

while the man who allegedly had sexual relations with her was freed because of the lack of four witnesses. Although such cases have come to represent *Sharia* in the West, many Muslims believe that these cases reflect a departure from the true spirit of *Sharia*. An editorial in the *Ghanaian Chronicle* read:

> Some so-called Muslim scholars have attempted to justify stoning on the grounds that it applies where the adulterers and fornicators are married. In any case, in the case of Amina Lawal and the Katsina Sharia court how come that no punishment was meted out to the man who made Amina Lawal pregnant? Why create the impression that there is no justice for women in Islam? Obviously at work was a combination of pre-Islamic practices, male chauvinism, sheer ignorance, and zealotry.[24]

A *Sharia* Court of Appeal overturned her conviction in 2003. According to four of the five judges, the original sentence had violated certain precepts of Islamic law because: it did not meet the requirement that three local judges hear her case — only one was present at the time of conviction; the defendant's right to proper legal defense was not provided;[25] and circumstantial evidence, in this case her pregnancy, was not considered sufficient evidence, according to Islamic law.[26]

The charges by scholars that Nigeria's Islamic court had misapplied Islamic law in the Lawal case reflect the plurality of interpretations within the Islamic legal tradition.

It is likely that Nigerian Muslims will continue to explore the flexibility built into *Sharia* as they develop their system of law. According to Gallup data, *Sharia* as a source of legislation today draws strong support from more than 7 in 10 Nigerian Muslims who say they want Sharia as at least a source of legislation — 1 in 5 wants it as the only source. At the same time, about 1 in 5 does not want it to be a source of legislation at all.

If the West and many Muslims want democracy for the Muslim world — seeing it as a stabilizing force and key to future progress — critical questions must be addressed:

- Why is democracy absent in so much of the Muslim world? Is Islam the problem?

- How do 1.3 billion Muslims view democracy?

- Should majority Muslim support for *Sharia* make the West panic?

- When Muslim men and women express a desire for *Sharia*, what do they mean?

- What is Muslim democratic thought?

- If democracy is a desired goal for many Muslims and for U.S. foreign policy, do Muslims believe the West has any role to play?

Why Is Democracy Absent in So Much of the Muslim World?

The answer to this question lies more in history and politics than in religion. We in the West had centuries to move from

Arbitrary borders and non-representative rulers produced weak nation-states with non-democratic governments that perpetuated a culture of authoritarianism.

monarchies to modern democratic states, from divine-right kingdoms to modern secular nation-states, and we suffered from revolutionary and civil wars in the process. In contrast, governments in the Muslim world, created after World War II, are only decades old.

Equally important, many Muslims lived for several centuries under European colonial rule. In the mid-20th century, when many countries became nation-states, their borders and unelected rulers were often selected or approved by colonial powers. In South Asia, the British divided the Indian subcontinent into India and (West and East) Pakistan shortly before granting their independence; the Muslim-majority state of Kashmir became part of India. Post-partition, the world witnessed communal warfare between Hindus and Muslims; the migration of millions, and subsequently, civil war between West and East Pakistan leading to the creation of Bangladesh; and conflicts in Kashmir over Indian rule that continue today.

In the Middle East, the French created the boundaries for what is now modern Lebanon, and the British set borders for Kuwait and Iraq and divided Palestine and Transjordan (later Jordan). Two Hashemite brothers from Arabia, Abdullah and Faisal, became kings of Jordan and Syria. Later, Faisal became king of Iraq. In 1950, Jordan formally annexed the West Bank, tripling the size of its population and creating a situation in which a minority Jordanian government ruled over the majority Palestinian population, who outnumbered the Jordanians by 2 to 1.[27] In the 1950s and 1960s, monarchs were overthrown, and military rulers or juntas replaced them in Egypt, Syria, Libya, and Iraq. Thus, the Middle East has been characterized by a lack of political stability for at least the last century. Many Muslim countries continue to be ruled by monarchies and by military or ex-military dictatorships.

Arbitrary borders and non-representative rulers produced weak nation-states with non-democratic governments that perpetuated a culture of authoritarianism. Non-government organizations that are key to supporting democracy (political parties, trade unions, educational and social services, professional and human rights organizations, and the media) were state-controlled or nonexistent. Many countries also suffered from failed economies and political corruption. Numerous critics argue that Europe and America turned a blind eye to such conditions, supporting autocrats in the Muslim world and elsewhere to gain their allegiance during the Cold War and — in the Middle East — to ensure access to oil.

Iran is an example of the complex effects of European imperialism. Although Iran was never formally colonized, both Russia and Britain vied for influence in that country. The British and the Soviets placed a very young Mohammad Reza Pahlavi on the throne, replacing his father as shah. In 1951, the Iranian parliament and the popular, democratically elected Prime Minister Mohammad Mossadegh nationalized Iran's oil industry. The intelligence agencies of Great Britain and the United States successfully removed Mossadegh from power in a 1953 coup, and the country moved toward autocracy under the shah. The coup's repercussions and its contribution to anti-Americanism would be felt during Iran's Islamic Revolution of 1979 and the occupation of the American embassy.[28]

Like most Muslim governments, Iran looked to the West for its expertise and models of development. Thus, Western experts and modernizing Muslim elites adopted the dominant Western paradigm for development: "Every day, in every way, things should become more Western/secular." This formula led to the adoption of Western secular, political, economic, and educational institutions and lifestyles. To be modern was not simply a matter of technology transfer. It was to be *Westernized* — wear modern (that is, Western) dress; speak a modern (Western) language; go to a secular school or university with a modern (Western-based) curriculum; and build modern cities and neighborhoods, often designed by Western architects. The presuppositions of modernization theory were captured in the title of Daniel Lerner's *The Passing of Traditional Society*. Many believed that Muslims had to choose "Mecca or mechanization."[29]

In a survey conducted in 2006 by American University, a 21-year-old Muslim student from Kenya said, "The greatest change in my society has been a large-scale Westernization . . . Americanization, of the community. Mostly it affects the young people, from the way they think to the way they dress and act." Describing the changes between his and his parents' generation, he continued:

It has become rarer now to find a person as well versed in his own language as he is versed in the English language. Societal values are being lost as the people race to that which they see as better, with immorality, alcoholism, and such vices on the rise. It is becoming harder to find someone well versed in his religion in a community that once produced great scholars . . . a gradual but sure alienation of people from what is truly theirs.[30]

The Iranian Revolution of 1979 blindsided experts and shocked the Western world. Who could explain the fall of the powerful Western-dressed, English-speaking shah — the father of Iran's modernizing White Revolution? Iran had an ambitious, well-funded modernization campaign, a modern-educated elite, a powerful military, strong ties to America and Europe, and major oil-producing power. The shah's opponents, who had no significant weapons, relied on religious rhetoric and a mosque network to organize and mobilize and were led by a bearded, aging ayatollah living in exile in a Paris suburb. Yet, they achieved victory in a comparatively "bloodless" Islamic revolution.

Almost unnoticed, Islam's presence in politics had been sharply reasserted from Libya and Sudan to Pakistan and Malaysia. Governments' political, military, and economic failures caused widespread disillusionment with their excessive dependence on the West. This "Westoxification" was condemned for robbing Muslims of their source of identity and values, and thus their unity and strength. Islamic movements and leaders, many of whom were modern educated, called for a return to the "straight path" of Islam — the alternative to Western capitalism and Soviet Marxism and socialism.

According to a 2003 *Christian Science Monitor* article, Lies Marcoes, who worked with Islamic organizations for the Asia

Foundation in Jakarta, reported a clear shift among Indonesians toward Islam as a response to the failure of their government. "Many people see the failure of the government to make cleaner government, stop vice, and help the poor, and so some will turn to sharia as the answer," she said.[31]

For example, Ali Achmad, a 26-year-old teacher at Pesantren Al Kamal in Jakarta, told *The Christian Science Monitor* that he voted for the staunchly secular Megawati Sukarnoputri in the 1999 election because he thought she would end the government's infamous corruption and help Indonesia's downtrodden. However, Achmad said he had become extremely disappointed in Indonesia's secular government: "This government is a total failure; they haven't embraced reform or protected our rights. There's gambling and prostitution everywhere. I'm so disappointed." Achmad said he intended to vote for the Prosperous Justice Party, which favors strict Islamic law for Indonesia over the country's secular arrangements, in the 2004 election. "Islamic law would wipe out corruption. It seems like the only solution to our problems," he said.[32]

A 21-year-old Kenyan university student in Turkey said:

> Islam has come across and conquered great obstacles proving again and again that we were told the truth when they said that the religion is Islam. It has provided the basis of every great human achievement, the solution to every unsolvable human problem. But at some point, we lost all that. A good thing is like gold; if you never put it into a fire and heat it, it never gets that luster that makes it gold. Such

> *Within the last several years, religious parties in the Arab world have decisively defeated their secular opponents, as Islamist candidates have proved successful at the polls.*

is Islam, a good thing so it has to go through fire if it is to discover its essence.[33]

Faithfulness to God's message and mission, many argued, had produced vast empires and civilizations, starting with the Islamic community in the 7th century and spanning much of the world until the dawn of European colonialism in the 18th century. Wealthy oil states such as Libya, Saudi Arabia, and other Gulf states used Islam and their oil wealth to promote their influence globally. Fears of "radical Islamic fundamentalism" — manifest in Iran's export of revolutionary Islam; in extremist groups such as the Egyptian Islamic Jihad, the assassins of Egypt's President Anwar Sadat; and in the rise of Palestinian Islamic Jihad — dominated the 1980s. But what observers missed was the "quiet revolution," the existence of mainstream, non-violent Islamic political and social movements that sought power and reform through ballots, not bullets.

In the late 1980s and 1990s, amid massive pressure from public protests over failed economies, Muslim governments held limited and state-controlled elections. Voters went to the polls, in some countries for the first time, and stunned everyone when Islamic candidates and parties emerged as the leading opposition. Islamists proved successful political players, elected as presidents, prime ministers, mayors, parliamentarians, cabinet members, and speakers of national assemblies in countries as diverse as Egypt, Morocco, Turkey, Pakistan, Kuwait, Bahrain, Saudi Arabia, Iraq, Afghanistan, Malaysia, and Indonesia.

A Washington Post/ABC News poll in 2006 found that nearly half of Americans have a negative view of Islam, seven percentage points higher than observed a few months after Sept. 11, 2001.

Within the last several years, religious parties in the Arab world have decisively defeated their secular opponents, as Islamist candidates have proved successful at the polls. In Iraq's general elections in late 2005, the religious Shiite alliance won 128 of 275 seats.[34] In the Palestinian territories' first elections in a decade, Hamas overwhelmingly defeated the secular ruling party, Fatah. In Egypt, the outlawed Muslim Brotherhood won an unprecedented one-fifth of parliament's seats. In Turkey, the Justice and Development Party (AKP) won a landslide victory in the November 2002 parliamentary elections — something of a rarity in the secular republic. The AKP won a majority in parliament, 363 seats, which was just four short of the plurality needed to rewrite the constitution drawn up by the secular vanguard army generals after the coup in 1980.[35] Islamists performed strongly in Saudi Arabia's 2005 polls, with moderate Islamists winning all the seats on the municipal councils in the cities of Mecca and Medina.[36]

However, the situation has recently changed. Post 9/11, rulers from Egypt to Uzbekistan are using the threat of al-Qaeda and global terrorism to brand any and all opposition as extremist, to control elections, and to legitimize their authoritarian governments. For example, although Egyptian President Hosni Mubarak promised to repeal Egypt's infamous emergency laws when he ran for re-election in Egypt's first-ever contested presidential election in 2005, he reneged on the promise because of "security" concerns. Egyptians must remember that they live in an inflamed region, said Mubarak. "We have to appreciate that Egypt, from time to time, is targeted."[37] The emergency laws, which have been in place since Mubarak came to power in 1981, allow arbitrary arrests and detentions.

Is Islam the Problem? Competing Images in the West and the Muslim World

The failures of governments, the hijacking of Islam by rulers and by terrorists, as well as assassinations, suicide attacks, and abuse of women and minorities have taken their toll on Muslim societies and on the image of Islam in the West.

A *Washington Post*/ABC News poll in 2006 found that nearly half of Americans — 46% — have a negative view of Islam, seven percentage points higher than observed a few months after Sept. 11, 2001.[38] According to the poll, the proportion of Americans who believe that Islam helps stoke violence against non-Muslims has more than doubled since the 9/11 attacks, from 14% in January 2002 to 33%. Similarly, a Pew Research Center survey found that about a third of Americans (36%) say Islam is more likely than other religions to encourage violence among its followers.[39]

In contrast, the majority in the Muslim world see Islam through different eyes — as a moderate, peaceful religion that is central to their self-understanding and their success. As we saw in the last chapter, overwhelming numbers of Muslims continue to identify religion as a primary marker of their identity, a source of guidance and strength, and crucial to their progress.

> *While acknowledging and admiring many aspects of Western democracy, those surveyed do not favor wholesale adoption of Western models of democracy.*

With the exception of Kazakhstan, majorities of those surveyed in Gallup Polls of countries with substantial Muslim populations (as high as 98% in Egypt, 96% in Indonesia, and 86% in Turkey) say that religion is an important part of their daily lives. This compares with 68% of respondents in the United States and only 28% of respondents in the United Kingdom for whom religion is an important part of their daily lives.

Yet, democracy is among the most frequent responses given as a key to a more just society and to progress. As a result, when asked to comment on aspects of life that are important to them, significant numbers of respondents cite both having an enriched religious and spiritual life and a democratically elected government as at least very important.

How Do 1.3 Billion Muslims View Democracy?

Cutting across diverse Muslim countries, social classes, and gender differences, answers to our questions reveal a complex and surprising reality. Substantial majorities in nearly all nations surveyed (95% in Burkina Faso, 94% in Egypt, 93% in Iran, and 90% in Indonesia) say that if drafting a constitution for a new country, they would guarantee freedom of speech, defined as "allowing all citizens to express their opinion on the political, social, and economic issues of the day."

However, while acknowledging and admiring many aspects of Western democracy, those surveyed do not favor wholesale

> *In the United States, a 2006 Gallup Poll indicates that a majority of Americans want the Bible as a source of legislation.*

adoption of Western models of democracy. Many appear to want their own democratic model that incorporates *Sharia* — and not one that is simply dependent on Western values. Actually, few respondents associate "adopting Western values" with Muslim political and economic progress. Abuses in the name of *Sharia* have not led to wholesale rejection of it.

In our data, the emphasis that those in substantially Muslim countries give to a new model of government — one that is democratic yet embraces religious values — helps to explain why majorities in most countries, with the exception of a handful of nations, want *Sharia* as at least "a" source of legislation.[40]

- In only a few countries did a majority say that *Sharia* should have no role in society; yet in most countries, only a minority want *Sharia* as "the only source" of law. In Jordan, Egypt, Pakistan, Afghanistan, and Bangladesh, majorities want *Sharia* as the "only source" of legislation.

- Most surprising is the absence of systemic differences in many countries between males and females in their support for *Sharia* as the only source of legislation. For example, in Jordan, 54% of men and 55% of women want *Sharia* as the only source of legislation. In Egypt, the percentages are 70% of men and 62% of women; in Iran, 12% of men and 14% of women; and in Indonesia, 14% of men and 14% of women.

Significant majorities in many countries say religious leaders should play no direct role in drafting a country's constitution or deciding how women dress in public.

Ironically, we don't have to look far from home to find a significant number of people who want religion as a source of law. In the United States, a 2006 Gallup Poll indicates that a majority of Americans want the Bible as a source of legislation.[41]

- Forty-six percent of Americans say that the Bible should be "a" source, and 9% believe it should be the "only" source of legislation.

- Perhaps even more surprising, 42% of Americans want religious leaders to have a direct role in writing a constitution, while 55% want them to play no role at all. These numbers are almost identical to those in Iran.

Should Majority Support for *Sharia* Make the West Panic?

Sharia has been equated with stoning of adulterers, chopping off limbs for theft, imprisonment or death in blasphemy and apostasy cases, and limits on the rights of women and minorities. The range of differing perceptions about *Sharia* surfaced in Iraq when Shia leaders, such as Iraq's senior Shiite cleric Grand Ayatollah Ali al-Sistani, called for an Islamic democracy, including *Sharia* as a basis of law in Iraq's new constitution.

An Iraqi Christian member of the Iraqi constitution's drafting committee, Yonadam Kanna, said in summer 2005 that the consequences of making *Sharia* one of the main sources of law would be dire. "For women it would be a disaster."[42] Nevertheless, more than 1,000 Iraqi women rallied in support of *Sharia* in the southern city of Basra in August 2005 in response to another rally opposing *Sharia* in Baghdad a week earlier.

Taking a stance on the debate regarding the role of *Sharia* in Iraq's new constitution, then-administrator L. Paul Bremer in 2004 said of the interim constitution, "Our position is clear. It can't be law until I sign it."[43] Donald Rumsfeld, then-Secretary of Defense, warned in 2003 that the United States would not allow Iraq to become a theocracy like Iran, confusing the idea of including *Sharia* in Iraq's new constitution with creating a theocracy, or clerical rule.[44]

Although in many quarters, *Sharia* has become the buzzword for religious rule, responses to the Gallup Poll indicate that wanting *Sharia* does not automatically translate into wanting theocracy. Significant majorities in many countries say religious leaders should play no direct role in drafting a country's constitution, writing national legislation, drafting new laws, determining foreign policy and international relations, or deciding how women dress in public or what is televised or published in newspapers. Others who opt for a direct role tend to stipulate that religious leaders should only serve in an advisory capacity to government officials.

In the West, *Sharia* often evokes an image of a restrictive society where women are oppressed and denied basic human rights. Indeed, women have suffered under government-imposed *Sharia* regulations in Muslim countries such as Pakistan, Sudan, the

> *While **Sharia** is commonly depicted as a rigid and oppressive legal system, Muslim women tend to have a more nuanced view of **Sharia**, viewing it as compatible with their aspirations for empowerment.*

Taliban's Afghanistan, Saudi Arabia, and Iran. However, those who want *Sharia* often charge that these regulations are un-Islamic interpretations.

Gallup Poll data show us that most respondents want women to have autonomy and equal rights. Majorities of respondents in most countries surveyed believe that women should have:

- the same legal rights as men (85% in Iran; 90% range in Indonesia, Bangladesh, Turkey, and Lebanon; 77% in Pakistan; and 61% in Saudi Arabia). Surprisingly, Egypt (57%) and Jordan (57%), which are generally seen as more liberal, lag behind Iran, Indonesia, and other countries.

- rights to vote: 80% in Indonesia, 89% in Iran, 67% in Pakistan, 90% in Bangladesh, 93% in Turkey, 56% in Saudi Arabia, and 76% in Jordan say women should be able to vote without any influence or interference from family members.

- the right to hold any job for which they are qualified outside the home. Malaysia, Mauritania, and Lebanon have the highest percentage (90%); Egypt (85%), Turkey (86%), and Morocco (82%) score in the 80% range, followed by Iran (79%), Bangladesh (75%), Saudi Arabia (69%), Pakistan (62%), and Jordan (61%).

- the right to hold leadership positions at cabinet and national council levels. While majorities in the countries surveyed support this statement, respondents in Saudi Arabia (40%) and Egypt (50%) are the exceptions.

While *Sharia* is commonly depicted as a rigid and oppressive legal system, Muslim women tend to have a more nuanced view of *Sharia*, viewing it as compatible with their aspirations for empowerment. For example, Jenan al-Ubaedy, one of the 90 women who sat on Iraq's National Assembly in early 2005, told *The Christian Science Monitor* that she supported the implementation of *Sharia*. However, she said that as an assembly member, she would fight for women's right for equal pay, paid maternity leave, and reduced hours for pregnant women. She said she also planned to encourage women to wear *hijab* and focus on strengthening their families. To Ubaedy, female empowerment is consistent with Islamic values.[45]

When Muslim Men and Women Express a Desire for *Sharia*, What Do They Mean?

A common misconception about what *Sharia* is and means accounts for both religious militants' inflexibility and many non-Muslims' fears. Historically, many Muslims and non-Muslims have come to confuse and use the terms *Sharia* and *Islamic law* interchangeably. Because the Quran is not a law book, early jurists used revelation as well as reason to create a body of laws to govern their societies. But, over time, these man-made laws came to be viewed as sacred and unchangeable.

Muslims who want to see *Sharia* as a source of law in constitutions therefore have very different visions of how that would manifest. Though the definition of *Sharia* refers to the principles in the Quran and prophetic tradition, some expect full implementation of classical or medieval Islamic law; others want a more restricted approach, like prohibiting alcohol, requiring the head of state to be a Muslim, or creating *Sharia* courts to hear cases involving Muslim family law (marriage, divorce, and inheritance). Still others simply want to ensure that no constitutional law violates the principles and values of Islam, as found in the Quran.

To clarify the distinction between *Sharia* and "Islamic law," think of *Sharia* as a compass (God's revelation, timeless principles that cannot change) and Islamic law (*fiqh*) as a map. This map must conform to the compass, but it reflects different times, places, and geography. The compass is fixed; the map is subject to change.

Many reformers claim that the challenge today is distinguishing what comes directly from the Quran (rituals for prayer, fasting, pilgrimage) and is universally binding, from scholarly interpretation of revelation (specific regulations regarding marriage or divorce, and so on) that varies within specific social contexts. The challenge is to differentiate the time-specific and the timeless.

Muslim reformers today argue that Islamic law should be reviewed in light of changing social circumstances. For example, Sisters in Islam, a Malaysian-based NGO for women's rights, lobbied the Malaysian government to impose restrictions on polygamous marriages. Citing Quranic verses and prophetic traditions, the NGO advocated women's right to list a polygamy condition in their marriage contracts. If a husband decides

A fatwa, however, is a non-binding legal opinion, and Muslims choose which fatwa they will and will not apply to their lives. In this regard, Muslims participate in a "free market" of religious thought.

to marry a second woman, he would then be legally bound to divorce his first wife and pay her deferred dowry and alimony.

When some Islamic legal scholars (*muftis*) accused the NGO of violating "Islamic law," the NGO charged back with Quranic verses and prophetic traditions that establish monogamy as the norm. They also cited that the Prophet Muhammad's own great-granddaughter, Sakina binte Hussain, put various conditions in her marriage contract, including the condition that her husband could not marry another woman if he wanted to remain married to her. In a press release, the NGO wrote:

> It is therefore clear that giving a wife such an option for obtaining a divorce through the marriage contract or *ta'liq* is not against Islamic teachings. It is not a new interpretation which has only arisen in these modern times. On the contrary, it is supported by traditional practices from the early days of Islam.[46]

This example provides a glimpse into the wide and diverse range of interpretations that characterize Islamic law. Thus, when Muslims say they support the application of *Sharia*, what that means can drastically vary from one person to another.

The issue of religion and change is not peculiar to Islam; people of all faiths contend with it. Sacred texts or classical formulations of law do not contain specific solutions for many modern problems. Are cloning and in vitro fertilization Islamically acceptable? Can a woman be president of a modern nation-state? How should banks and financial houses handle interest and loans? What dispensations are allowed for Muslims living as minorities? Are preemptive military strikes ever justified?

With no clear text in the Quran and no central religious authority, the expert legal opinions (*fatawa*) that *muftis* give can differ substantially depending on how conservative or reform-minded and how politicized or apolitical they are as individuals. In the end, legal answers depend on who your *mufti* is just as the advice from your rabbi or your minister depends on who he or she is. A *fatwa*, however, is a non-binding legal opinion, and Muslims choose which *fatwa* they will and will not apply to their lives. In this regard, Muslims participate in a "free market" of religious thought — a flexibility that may account for both the resilience and diversity of Islam across time and geography.

What Is Muslim Democratic Thought?

There are different schools of thought among Muslims regarding democracy and Islam. A minority opinion, in Islamic literature, is that "democracy" is a foreign concept. People who hold this view — including mainstream Muslims and extremists — want to restore an Islamic empire because they say that popular sovereignty is idolatry and denies God's supreme power.

However, as results from the Gallup Poll respondents show, support for democratic freedoms and women's rights is widespread in the Muslim world. There are a number of principles in the Islamic tradition that support these freedoms.

Sudanese intellectual and former diplomat Abdelwahab El-
Affendi argues that Islam's emphasis on monotheism and God's
absolute power requires a democratic system: "The sovereignty
of one man contradicts the sovereignty of God, for all men
are equal in front of God. . . . Blind obedience to one-man
rule is contrary to Islam."[47] Monotheism in Islam includes the
belief that life cannot be compartmentalized; religion cannot be
separated from all aspects of life, as in the banning of religion
from the public sphere.[48]

Iran's former President Mohammad Khatami, an advocate of
Islamic democracy, said in a June 2001 television interview that
"today, world democracies are suffering from a major vacuum
which is the vacuum of spirituality" and that Islam can provide
the framework combining democracy with spirituality and religious government.

Like Jews and Christians, Muslims reinterpret their tradition
to support modern forms of democracy, which can vary a great
deal. Forms of Western democracy have included presidential,
parliamentary, and proportional representation; direct and indirect elections of leaders; and consensual and adversarial forms
of government. Similarly, although the United States has insisted on the separation of church and state, several European
democracies such as Great Britain, Germany, and Norway have
a state religion and/or provide state funding or support for officially recognized religious institutions. Despite France's strict
separation of church and state based on its 1905 Law of Separation, the government provides funding for churches, tem-
ples, and synagogues built before 1905 in the name of cultural

Majorities of respondents disagree with the statement that "the U.S. is serious about encouraging the establishment of democratic systems of government in this region."

preservation. Although these buildings are considered state property and are maintained by national and municipal governments, the clergy can use them for free. Furthermore, since 1959, the French government has provided subsidies directly to all private schools — many of which are Catholic — and often pays the salaries of teachers in those schools.[49]

Fundamental to the process of adapting to new circumstances is the Islamic concept of interpretation (*ijtihad*) — the exercise of informed, independent legal judgment. As Khurshid Ahmad, a prominent Islamic leader in Britain and a Pakistani parliamentarian, said: "God has revealed only broad principles . . . It is through the *ijtihad* that people of every age try to implement and apply divine guidance to the problems of their times."[50]

Other Islamic concepts that legitimate Muslim versions of democracy arguably include the idea of consultation (*shura*) between the government and the people in the selection or election of rulers. This idea, coupled with community consensus (*ijma*), a source of Islamic law, is now used to support modern parliaments and national assemblies as a way to reflect the collective judgment of the community.

While vigorous debates about democracy continue, change is taking place on the ground. However slowly and haltingly, many governments are responding to pressures for more political participation and elections with varying degrees of openness, freedom, and transparency.

If Democracy Is a Desired Goal for Many Muslims and for U.S. Foreign Policy, Do Muslims Believe the West Has Any Role to Play?

To answer this question, we need to look at some sobering realities. There are a number of challenges in the plan to win the minds and hearts of Muslims; feedback to multiple questions in the Gallup Poll reflects criticisms and skepticism about U.S. foreign policies and actions. Although there was widespread desire for democracy, which many Muslims view as necessary for their progress, with the exception of 10 countries surveyed,[51] majorities disagree with the statement that "the U.S. is serious about encouraging the establishment of democratic systems of government in this region."

Muslim attitudes toward the United States have been affected by what is perceived as America's — and to a great extent Europe's — "double standard" in promoting democracy: its long track record of supporting authoritarian regimes and failure to promote democracy in the Muslim world as it did in other areas and countries after the fall of the Soviet Union.

In a major policy address in 2002, Ambassador Richard Haass, a former senior State Department official in the George W. Bush administration, remarked that before the invasion of Iraq, both Democratic and Republican administrations practiced "democratic exceptionalism" in the Muslim world, subordinating democracy to other national interests such as accessing oil, containing the Soviet Union, and grappling with the Arab-Israeli conflict.[52]

More recently, Muslim cynicism about the United States promoting democracy has grown for a number of reasons: the use of "creating democracy" as a retroactive rationale for invading Iraq only after weapons of mass destruction in that country didn't materialize; the impression that the United States was orchestrating an "acceptable" American version of democracy in Iraq with its own hand-picked "George Washington," Ahmed Chalabi; and the trail of human rights abuses from Guantanamo to Abu Ghraib. U.S. and European refusal to recognize the democratically elected Hamas government in Palestine further reinforces such impressions.

"They (U.S. officials) are all for democracy as long as they like the results," Kenneth Roth, head of Human Rights Watch, told *The Financial Times*. Roth believes that America's mission to promote democracy has become equated with "regime change" and has lost credibility in the Muslim world. "Its push for democracy is over now," he said.[53]

In *The Washington Post*, Salameh Nematt, a Jordanian analyst and former Washington bureau chief for the Arabic-language newspaper *al-Hayat*, echoed Roth's pessimism:

It's a success story for al-Qaeda, a success story for autocratic Arab regimes that made democracy look ugly in their people's eyes. They can say to their people: "Look at the democracy that the Americans want to bring to you. Democracy is trouble. You may as well forget about what the Americans promise you. They promise you death."[54]

Worldwide Muslim opinions have been influenced by the explosion in mass communications that has swept across much of the Muslim world and outstripped the control of governments. Newspapers such as *Asharq Al-Awsat* and *Al-Hayat* have joined TV networks like al-Jazeera, Al-Arabiyya, MBC, and others to become alternatives to CNN and BBC. The information revolution's effect can be seen in Saudi Arabia, where large numbers classify international television (82%), newspapers (65%), international radio (42%), and the Internet (32%) as "very important" sources for being well-informed on international affairs. When asked whether they had watched al-Jazeera within the past seven days, three-quarters of Saudis say they had watched the satellite news channel — drawn by its "on-site," "objective," and "daring" reporting.

What Do Muslims Believe the Chances Are of Improving Relations With the West?

The West's concern for better relations with the Arab/Muslim world tends to be perceived most positively in the African nations surveyed. At 64%, Sierra Leoneans are the most likely of all populations studied to say that the West shows concern. The picture is starkly different in most predominantly Muslim Asian and Middle Eastern countries, where populations are far more likely to think that the West does not show concern than does show concern. Negative sentiment is highest in Turkey, where 64% say that the West doesn't show concern for better relations; 57% of Egyptians and 53% of Kuwaitis say that the West doesn't exhibit concern.

Among the top responses to "What do you admire least about the West?" is hatred or degradation of Islam and Muslims.

Despite the harsh feedback, do Muslims want better relations with the West? In most countries, the percentage who say that a better understanding between Western and Muslim cultures concerns them a lot significantly outnumbers percentages who say that it does not concern them. In some cases, as with Saudi Arabia, Morocco, and Lebanon, those who are concerned outnumber those who are not by a ratio of 2 to 1.

But what do respondents believe the West can do to improve relations with the Muslim world? From Morocco to Indonesia, the most frequent responses to this open-ended question are:

- demonstrate more respect; more consideration

- do not underestimate the status of Arab/Muslim countries

- demonstrate more understanding of Islam as a religion, and do not downgrade what Islam stands for

Equally revealing, among the top responses to "What do you admire least about the West?" is hatred or degradation of Islam and Muslims. But how do these answers relate to issues of freedom and democracy?

Respondents were asked: "Suppose someone from the government of the United States were to ask you in private what was the most important thing the United States could do to improve the quality of life of people like you in this country. What would your recommendation be?" The most common responses, after "reduce unemployment and improve the economic infra-structure," are "stop interfering in the internal affairs of Arab/Islamic states," "stop imposing your beliefs and policies," "respect our political rights and stop controlling us," and "give us our own freedom."

Taking a closer look at what we will term the "Muslim democrats"[55] — those who believe that democracy is important to their progress and future — enhances our understanding of the issue. Perhaps this group's most interesting characteristic is its strong emphasis on religion and women's rights.

- A majority of Muslim democrats say that having a rich spiritual life is essential, something they cannot live without, and more than 60% say that they attended a religious service in the past seven days.

- Majorities support women having: the same legal rights as men (78%); the rights to vote without family interference (88%), hold a job for which they are qualified (82%), hold leadership positions in cabinets and national assemblies (72%), and drive a car (67%).

Interestingly, Muslim democrats are more concerned about better relations with the West but more likely to view the United States unfavorably and to say that Western societies do not show concern for better coexistence with the Arab/Muslim world. These perceptions are reflected in the small percentages (5% to 10%) who believe that the United States is trustworthy, friendly, or treats other countries respectfully.

Given these perceptions, as well as the belief by many that the West is antagonistic toward Islam and Muslims, perhaps one of the lessons is that when it comes to democracy, the rule of law, and human rights, the standards that the West applies to itself must be seen as consistent with those expected and demanded of others.

KEY POINTS:

* Although democracies are rare in Muslim countries, many Muslims value a number of democratic principles.

* In general, Muslims see no contradiction between democratic values and religious principles.

* Overall, Muslims want neither a theocracy nor a secular democracy and would opt for a third model in which religious principles and democratic values coexist.

* Men and women support a role for *Sharia* as a source of legislation, and at the same time, most do not want religious leaders directly in charge of drafting legislation.

Chapter 3: **What Makes a Radical?**

THE WAR AGAINST global terrorism has been waging for more than six years, yet Muslim extremism and violence continue to grow. Attacks are sweeping across the world from North Africa to Southeast Asia, with targets extending from Casablanca, Madrid, and London to Istanbul, Riyadh, Jakarta, and Bali. The Osama bin Ladens of the world have turned a once-popular *jihad* — a struggle in Afghanistan against Soviet occupation supported by the Muslim world and the West — into an unholy war of suicide bombings, hostage taking, and broad-based terror.

At the same time, Islamophobia has increased sharply in Europe and America, while anti-Americanism continues to spread in the Arab and Muslim worlds. In the West, we are galvanized by terrorist attacks and suicide bombings in Iraq, Israel, Palestine, Afghanistan, Pakistan, and Indonesia, while the Muslim world is galvanized by the invasion and occupation of Iraq, abuses at Abu Ghraib and Guantanamo, and images of civilian deaths and destruction from the Israeli invasions of Gaza and southern Lebanon.

It is against this backdrop that the United States desires stable, secular democracies in the Muslim countries it views as supporting terrorism, with the successful creation of such democracies being the ultimate measure of victory in the "war on terrorism."

U.S. and European leaders speak of a war of ideas in which it is critical to win the hearts and minds of Muslims. But a number of challenges must be overcome before that can be achieved. In a deteriorating atmosphere in which the clarion call of a clash of civilizations seems more inevitable, what can be done? The need for public diplomacy has never been more important, making solid data about those whom we wish to convince even more important.

Former U.S. Defense Secretary Robert McNamara says he now believes that what doomed the United States during the Vietnam War was that it knew almost nothing about its enemy, the North Vietnamese.[56] The United States didn't know what the enemy thought or what they wanted. The war was seen only in broad, geopolitical terms — part of the "domino theory," the worldwide struggle to prevent the spread of a monolithic communism, just as the present war is cast as a war against global terrorism (that some Muslims see as a war against Islam).[57]

As the world community continues to struggle with global terrorism, it is essential that we look closer and understand "the other," both the moderate, Muslim mainstream majority and the extremist minority — those who are or could someday be linked with extremism and terrorism. Some of the key questions that must be asked, and to some degree have been answered by the Gallup study, are:

- Who are the political radicals?

- What is the link between terrorism and poverty or ignorance?

The conventional wisdom has often fallen back on an intuitive sense that a combination of religious fanaticism, poverty, and unemployment drive extremism and terrorism.

- What is the relationship between Islam and terrorism? What about *jihad* and suicide terrorism?

- Why do they hate us and our way of life?

  - How do political radicals feel about our freedoms and technology?

  - What do they say about Western countries and leaders?

  - How do they view America?

- What are the primary drivers of radicalism?

Who Are the Political Radicals?

For decades, scholars and pundits have been debating about how terrorists and extremists are created. The causes of terrorism are said to be psychological (terrorists are abnormal, deranged, irrational), sociological (they lack education, are alienated social misfits), economic (they're poor, unemployed, hopeless), political (they reject democracy, freedom, human rights), and religious (they're fanatics, zealots, believers in a violent religion that rejects modernization and technology).

The conventional wisdom, based on old and deeply held stereotypes and presuppositions about extremists, has often fallen back on an intuitive sense that a combination of religious fanaticism, poverty, and unemployment drive extremism and terrorism. Reluctance to see extremists as otherwise intelligent, rational people responding to perceived grievances was apparent within weeks after 9/11. Media reported the "stunning discovery" that many of the attackers were not from the poor, downtrodden, undereducated, and alienated sectors of society, but that they, like their al-Qaeda leaders Osama bin Laden and Dr. Ayman al-Zawahiri, were well-educated, middle to upper class, and from stable family backgrounds. This profile raises important questions about why people from seemingly normal backgrounds become terrorists.

But, should the profiles of the 9/11 attackers, as well as al-Qaeda and other terrorist group leaders, have surprised us so much? Not if we had remembered recent history. Muslim extremism is not a new phenomenon.   *ce not US caused?*

Extremist groups from Egypt and Algeria to Lebanon, Pakistan, Indonesia, and the southern Philippines have existed for decades. Early studies by the Egyptian sociologist Saad Eddin Ibrahim and others of the assassins of Egypt's President Anwar Sadat in 1981 concluded:

> The typical social profile of members of militant Islamic groups could be summarized as being young (early twenties), of rural or small town backgrounds, from middle and lower middle class, with high achievement motivation, upwardly mobile, with science or engineering education, and from a normally cohesive family ... Most of those we investigated would be considered model young Egyptians.[58]

Similarly, with some exceptions, today's breed of militants and terrorists — from the 9/11 attackers to the London bombers

> *According to media reports, many of the 9/11 hijackers themselves exhibited behaviors hardly practiced by a religious Muslim.*

of 7/7 — have been educated individuals from middle-class and working-class backgrounds. Some were devout; others were not. For example, according to media reports, many of the 9/11 hijackers themselves exhibited behaviors hardly practiced by a religious Muslim. A number of them drank heavily and frequented strip clubs and porn shops.

Most were not graduates of madrassas or seminaries, but of private or public schools and universities. Bin Laden was trained in management, economics, and engineering. Al-Zawahiri, a surgeon, and other al-Qaeda leaders, as well as those responsible for the World Trade Center and Pentagon attacks, like Mohammed Atta, were well-educated, middle-class professionals. British-born Omar Sheikh, who was convicted and sentenced to death for the kidnapping and murder of *Wall Street Journal* reporter Daniel Pearl, was educated at elite private schools including the London School of Economics.[59]

Understanding extremists and the nature of extremism requires a global perspective that extends beyond conflicting opinions of experts or anecdotes from the "Arab street." What do Muslims polled across the world have to say? How many Muslims hold extremist views? What are their hopes and fears? What are their priorities? What do they admire, and what do they resent?

According to the Gallup Poll, 7% of respondents[60] think that the 9/11 attacks were "completely" justified and view the United States unfavorably. Among those who believe that the 9/11 attacks were not justified, whom we'll call "moderates,"

40% are pro-United States, but 60% view the United States unfavorably.

Analyzing and comparing the answers of the 7% with the moderate majority produced some surprising results. By focusing on the 7%, whom we'll call "the politically radicalized" because of their radical political orientation, we are not saying that all in this group commit acts of violence. However, those with extremist views are a potential source for recruitment or support for terrorist groups. This group is also so committed to changing political conditions that they are more likely to view other civilian attacks as justifiable: 13% of the politically radicalized versus 1% of moderates say that attacks on civilians are "completely justified."

What is the age and gender of those with extremist views? They are younger, but not substantially: 49% are between the ages of 18 and 29; 41% of those with moderate views are in the same age range. Contrary to what some might expect, while political radicals are more likely to be male (62%), 37% are female. In addition, a minority of suicide bombers have been women.[61]

What Is the Link Between Terrorism and Poverty or Ignorance?

The *Arab Development Report of 2005* and many other studies of Muslim countries well document the existence of significant poverty and illiteracy. These problems are found in Palestinian refugee camps and in the slums of Algiers, Cairo, Baghdad, and Jakarta as well as in many other non-Muslim developing nations. Poverty and lack of information and skills necessary

*Neither unemployment nor job
status differentiate radicals
from moderates.*

for social mobility result from deep-seated economic and social problems that can generate broad-based discontent. But are lack of education and poverty key factors that distinguish those with extremist views from moderates? The data say no.

The politically radicalized, on average, are more educated than moderates: 67% of the politically radicalized have secondary or higher educations (versus 52% of moderates). Radicals are not more economically disadvantaged: 65% of the politically radicalized say they have average or above-average income, versus 55% of moderates.

Are Political Radicals Jobless and Hopeless?

Unemployment, like poverty, has been a major social problem from Algeria to Egypt and in Pakistan, Bangladesh, and Indonesia. Yet, neither unemployment nor job status differentiate radicals from moderates. No difference exists in the unemployment rate among the politically radicalized and moderates; both are approximately 20%.

And, among those who are employed, the politically radicalized hold jobs with greater responsibility: Almost half (47%) of the politically radicalized, versus 34% of the moderates, say they supervise other people at work.

Radicals are also not more hopeless than the mainstream. Larger percentages of radicals respond that they are more satisfied with their financial situations, standard of living, and quality of life: 64% of the politically radicalized, versus 55% of moderates, believe their standard of living is getting better.

Surprisingly, the politically radicalized are also, on average, more optimistic about their personal future than are moderates. A greater percentage of the politically radicalized (52% vs. 45% of moderates) believe they will be much better off in five years. However, as we shall see, while a larger percentage of those with extremist views are more optimistic about their own lives, they are generally more pessimistic about world affairs and international politics.

What Is the Religion-Terrorism Connection?

The religious language and symbolism that terrorists use tend to place religion at center stage. Many critics charge that global terrorism is attributable to Islam — a militant or violent religion — and terrorists who are particularly religious folks. For example, in a *Washington Times* commentary, author Sam Harris writes:

> It is time we admitted that we are not at war with "terrorism." We are at war with Islam. This is not to say that we are at war with all Muslims, but we are absolutely at war with the vision of life that is prescribed to all Muslims in the Koran. The only reason Muslim fundamentalism is a threat to us is because the fundamentals of Islam are a threat to us. Every American should read the Koran and discover the relentlessness with which non-Muslims are vilified in its pages. The idea that Islam is a "peaceful religion hijacked

by extremists" is a dangerous fantasy — and it is now a particularly dangerous fantasy for Muslims to indulge.[62]

Lawrence Auster of *FrontPage* magazine echoes this sentiment. He writes: "The problem is not 'radical' Islam but Islam itself, from which it follows that we must seek to weaken and contain Islam . . ."[63]

What do the data say? Does personal piety correlate with radical views? The answer is no. Large majorities of those with radical views and moderate views (94% and 90%, respectively) say that religion is an important part of their daily lives. And no significant difference exists between radicals and moderates in mosque attendance.

Gallup probed respondents further and actually asked those who condone and condemn extremist acts why they said what they did. The responses fly in the face of conventional wisdom. For example, in Indonesia, the largest Muslim majority country in the world, many of those who condemn terrorism cite humanitarian or religious justifications to support their response. For example, one woman says, "Killing one life is as sinful as killing the whole world," paraphrasing verse 5:32 in the Quran.

On the other hand, not a single respondent in Indonesia who condones the attacks of 9/11 cites the Quran for justification. Instead, this group's responses are markedly secular and worldly. For example, one Indonesian respondent says, "The U.S. government is too controlling toward other countries, seems like colonizing."

The real difference between those who condone terrorist acts and all others is about politics, not piety.

The real difference between those who condone terrorist acts and all others is about politics, not piety.

How then do we explain extremists' religious rhetoric? As our data clearly demonstrate, religion is the dominant ideology in today's Arab and Muslim world, just as secular Arab nationalism was in the days of Egyptian President Gamal Abdel Nasser. The Palestinian Liberation Organization — from its inception, a staunchly secular group — used secular Palestinian nationalism in its rhetoric to justify acts of violence and to recruit. Just as Arab nationalism was used in the 1960s, today religion is used to justify extremism and terrorism.

Examining the link between religion and terrorism requires a larger and more complex context. Throughout history, close ties have existed among religion, politics, and societies. Leaders have used and hijacked religion to recruit members, to justify their actions, and to glorify fighting and dying in a sacred struggle.

What About Islam and *Jihad*?

No word has come to popularly symbolize violence and terror in the name of Islam more than *jihad*, a term that is widely used and abused. *Jihad* was used in the Afghan resistance to Soviet occupation and has since been employed in just about every Muslim struggle of resistance and liberation as well as extremism and terrorism in Bosnia, Kosovo, Chechnya, Kashmir, Gaza, Lebanon, and Bali. Terrorists such as bin Laden, Abu Musab al-Zarqawi, the London bombers, and other extremists as well as, ironically, many non-Muslims, conflate *jihad* with a Muslim holy war against unbelievers. However, many observant Muslims counter that holy war is not Islamic, but rather a Christian term that originated during the Crusades.

As we discussed earlier, historically, *jihad* has had multiple and conflicting meanings. However, even when interpreted in militaristic terms, *jihad* is governed by certain conditions: it cannot be preemptive, it must be declared by a state or religious body, and it must not target civilians. To Muslims, the term *jihad* connotes honor and sacrifice for others. Thus, to use *jihad* interchangeably with *terrorism* is not only inaccurate, but also counterproductive. One thing is clear: Among Muslims globally, the concept of *jihad* is considerably more nuanced than the single sense in which Western commentators invariably invoke the term.

Religion and Politics: Yesterday and Today

Today, many may see linking religion and politics in Islam as unique and peculiar. However, throughout history, religion and politics have been linked in other religions. In Judaism, the conquest and settlement of the land of Israel was pursued under the direction of God; King David and King Solomon were anointed by God. In Christianity, kings and emperors were often crowned by the pope. The Crusades were fought as a divinely sanctioned holy war; as Pope Urban II declared, "It is the will of God."[64] "Crown and cross," imperial expansion, and Christian mission motivated the conquistadors and European colonialism. In Hinduism, kings upheld the divine order, and

> *Catholic, Lutheran, and Presbyterian activists have bombed gay bars, shot or killed abortion staff, and bombed their clinics.*

the doctrine of *dharma* supported the Hindu social class-caste system.

In recent decades, religion has become a significant factor in wars of liberation and resistance as well as in acts of terrorism throughout the world. We see this in conflicts between Sikhs and Hindus in India; Muslim Bosniaks, Croatian Catholics, and Orthodox Serbs in the former Yugoslavia; Christian, Muslim, and Druze militias in Lebanon's civil war; Catholic and Protestant militants in Northern Ireland; Muslims and Christians in Nigeria; and Muslim (Hamas and Islamic Jihad) and Jewish fundamentalists (the Gush Emuneim, Meir Kahane's Kach Party and Yigal Amir) in Israel and Palestine.

Closer to home, the vast majority of terrorist attacks on U.S. soil have been perpetrated by Christian terrorist groups in the past 15 years. Catholic, Lutheran, and Presbyterian activists have bombed gay bars, shot or killed abortion staff, and bombed their clinics. White Christian supremacy inspired the attacks on the Centennial Olympic Park in Atlanta and many other incidents. Timothy McVeigh used Christian cosmotheism, espoused by William Pierce, to justify bombing the Alfred P. Murrah Federal Building in Oklahoma City. However different, religions have become a means to legitimize holy and unholy struggles and wars.[65]

Religion and Suicide Terrorism

The most controversial and increasingly widespread form of terrorism has been suicide bombing, employed since the

> *While redressing real or perceived occupation and injustice, religious and secular groups alike often frame their terrorist acts within a powerful religious context.*

early 1980s as a major strategic weapon of resistance by Muslim militants as well as by the Tamil Tigers in Sri Lanka. Often, suicide bombings are attributed to religious fundamentalism or religious fanaticism, motivated by a holy war mentality and the promise of heavenly rewards for martyrs. But, while terrorists appeal to religion to recruit volunteers, is religion the key precipitator of terrorism?

Research on every suicide attack in the world from 1980 to 2004 reveals that foreign occupation has motivated nearly every case. Robert Pape, the author of *Dying to Win: The Logic of Suicide Terrorism*, says:

> The central fact is that overwhelmingly suicide-terrorist attacks are not driven by religion as much as they are by a clear strategic objective: to compel modern democracies to withdraw military forces from the territory that the terrorists view as their homeland. From Lebanon to Sri Lanka to Chechnya to Kashmir to the West Bank, every major suicide-terrorist campaign — more than 95% of all the incidents — has had as its central objective to compel a democratic state to withdraw.[66]

However, while redressing real or perceived occupation and injustice, religious and secular groups alike often frame their terrorist acts within a powerful religious context.

The Tamil Tigers, a Marxist-Leninist group whose main tactic is suicide bombings, has appealed to Tamil Hindu identity in their struggle against Sinhalese Buddhists in Sri Lanka to

achieve independence. Hamas originated primarily to resist Israeli occupation, but religion has been used to legitimize its
existence and its acts of terrorism. Even the al-Aqsa Martyrs'
Brigade, a secular Palestinian militia similar to Hamas, has used
religion to justify its suicide bombings. It chose the name al-
Aqsa (a major mosque and religious site in Jerusalem) and calls
its attacks "jihads" and its fallen "jihadists" or martyrs. Some
terrorists, such as the 9/11 hijackers, aren't particularly observant (they freely drank and so forth) but turn to religion (scripture and prayers) as they face death.

Lebanon, Madrid, and Iraq provide good examples from the
past two decades of suicide bombers' strategy, tactics, and objec-
tives. Although suicide attacks are said to have originated with
Hamas in the Israeli-Palestinian conflict, they actually first occurred in the Muslim world in Lebanon. The most devastating
attack was that attributed to Hezbollah in 1983 against the U.S.
Marine barracks in Beirut, which killed 241 American troops.
The diverse religious backgrounds of Hezbollah's suicide attackers exemplify the extent to which members of resistance
movements are not necessarily motivated by religion. In attacks
in Lebanon in the 1980s, the attackers included only eight
Muslim fundamentalists, plus three Christians and 27 commu-
nists and socialists.[67]

The political context changed in 1989 after the Taif Accords,
which signaled the end of the Lebanese civil war. Hezbollah
became a player in electoral politics. Although as a political
party, Hezbollah has a presence in the Lebanese parliament, it
refused to lay down its arms in the south of Lebanon, continu-
ing to fight Israeli occupation. The Israeli pullout in 2000 was

widely seen by many, particularly militant Islamists, as vindicating the tactical use of violence and suicide bombing.

In contrast to attacks in Lebanon and in many other countries, the 2004 bombing in Madrid was carried out by a group with ties to al-Qaeda, not against occupation in Spain, but to terrorize Spaniards before elections and thus defeat the incumbent prime minister who supported Iraq's invasion and occupation. (This strategy evidently succeeded; the new government withdrew Spanish troops from Iraq shortly after assuming power.) Similarly, according to Pape's research, two-thirds of al-Qaeda suicide terrorists from 1995 to early 2004 were from countries where the United States has had a heavy presence of combat troops since 1990.

Suicide terrorism was unknown in Iraq before the U.S.-led invasion and occupation. However, it became a widespread tactic used by Sunni and Shia militants in their sectarian conflicts over power and to end U.S. occupation. Pape says:

> Before our invasion, Iraq never had a suicide-terrorist attack in its history. Never. Since our invasion, suicide terrorism has been escalating rapidly with 20 attacks in 2003, 48 in 2004, and over 50 in just the first five months of 2005. Every year that the United States has stationed 150,000 combat troops in Iraq, suicide terrorism has doubled.[68]

If suicide terrorism is not simply driven by blind religious, ethnic, or cultural hatred, but by perceived or real injustices, then what is the answer to the ever-present question "Why do they hate us?"

Why Do They Hate Us and Our Way of Life?

This question, raised in the immediate aftermath of 9/11, looms large following continued suicide and other terrorist attacks and the dramatic growth of anti-Americanism. A common answer from some U.S. politicians and experts has been: "They hate our way of life, our freedom, democracy, and success."

Considering the broad-based anti-Americanism not only among radicals but also among a significant mainstream majority in the Muslim world (and indeed in many other parts of the world), this answer does not satisfy. Although there are many common grievances expressed in the Muslim world, do the politically radicalized and moderates differ in attitudes toward the West?

- When asked what they admire about the West, the politically radicalized and moderates mention these top three spontaneous responses: (1) technology; (2) the West's value system, hard work, self-responsibility, rule of law, cooperation; and (3) fair political systems, democracy, respect of human rights, freedom of speech, gender equality.

- Contrary to popular belief that extremists are anti-democracy, a significantly higher percentage of the politically radicalized (50% vs. 35% of moderates) say that "moving toward greater governmental democracy" will foster progress in the Arab/Muslim world.

Moreover, when considering relations between the Muslim world and the West, the politically radicalized do not simply

> *When considering relations between the Muslim world and the West, the politically radicalized do not simply reject the West.*

reject the West: No significant difference exists between the percentage of the politically radicalized and moderates who say that "better understanding between the West and Arab/Islamic cultures concerns me a lot."

And even more surprising, the politically radicalized are more likely than moderates to associate Arab/Islamic nations with an eagerness to have better relationships with the West: 58% of the politically radicalized (versus 44% of moderates) express this.

What Do Muslims Say About Western Countries and Leaders?

Although many in the West believe that anti-Americanism is tethered to a basic hatred of the West as well as deep West-East religious and cultural differences, respondents' assessments of individual Western countries reveal a different picture. Unfavorable opinions of the United States or Great Britain do not preclude a favorable attitude toward other Western countries such as France or Germany.

The politically radicalized are consistently more negative than are moderates in their opinions of all Western countries tested in the survey. However, there is a stark contrast in their views of individual Western nations. Even those who are politically radicalized consistently differentiate between countries and leaders and do not see a monolithic West. For example, while only a quarter of the politically radicalized have very unfavorable opinions of France (25%) and Germany (26%), this percentage jumps to 68% for Britain and 84% for the United States.

Unfavorable opinions of Western heads of state also vary significantly: 90% of the politically radicalized and 62% of moderates express absolute dislike for George W. Bush; 70% of the politically radicalized and 43% of moderates do not like former British Prime Minister Tony Blair "at all." That level of dislike does not extend to other Western leaders. For example, dislike of former French President Jacques Chirac is significantly lower: 39% among the politically radicalized and 24% among moderates.

Similarly, 81% of the politically radicalized and 67% of moderates describe the United States as aggressive, while few see France (7% of moderates and 9% of the politically radicalized) or Germany (8% of moderates and 9% of the politically radicalized) as aggressive. These data do not reflect an across-the-board blind hatred of Western culture among those who are politically radicalized.

How Do They View America?

In an op-ed piece in the *International Herald Tribune*, Carnegie scholar Fawas Gerges recounted an interview he had with a human rights advocate, Egyptian Hazem Salem, in Cairo. The activist, who is in his twenties, told Gerges, "Look at what America is doing in Iraq. America is using democracy as a mask to colonize Muslim lands and to steal our oil."

When Gerges reminded him that President George W. Bush advocates promoting democracy in the Arab world, Salem retorted, "No, he is promoting chaos and civil war."[69]

While the spread of democracy has been the stated goal of the United States, with few exceptions, majorities in virtually every nation with majority or sizable Muslim populations disagree that the United States is serious about the establishment of democratic systems in the region:

- Only 24% in Egypt and Jordan and 16% in Turkey agree that the United States is serious about establishing democratic systems.

- The largest groups in agreement are in Lebanon (54%), Sierra Leone (68%), and Afghanistan (53%).

The politically radicalized are skeptical and pessimistic about world affairs. The skepticism among Muslims in general regarding the United States and its promotion of democracy is intensified among the politically radicalized: While about half (52%) of moderates say they disagree that the United States is serious about supporting democracy in the region, almost three-fourths (72%) of the politically radicalized disagree.

As mentioned earlier in the discussion about democratic exceptionalism, many Muslims charge that the United States and the West in general have a double standard when it comes to promoting democracy and human rights in the Arab/Muslim world. "Whenever the Israelis strike the Palestinians, the international community and the U.N. turn a blind eye or keep

> *For the politically radicalized, their fear of Western control and domination, as well as their lack of self-determination, reinforce their sense of powerlessness.*

quiet," says Saleh Bayeri, a politician and Muslim community leader in Jos, Nigeria. "But when the Palestinians launch a counterattack, it is condemned by America, the U.K. and other friends of Israel as a terror attack. That is the problem. It shows that the West is biased in dealing with Muslims."[70]

One female college student at the American University of Cairo, a leading institution of Western education in the region, said in an interview with Gerges, "Bush has given Israel carte blanche to attack Palestinians and Lebanese. The war on terror is an open-ended war on Muslims."[71]

Nearly two-thirds (63%) of the politically radicalized disagree that the United States will allow people in the region to "fashion their own political future as they see fit without direct U.S. influence," while 48% of moderates express this view. For the politically radicalized, their fear of Western control and domination, as well as their lack of self-determination, reinforce their sense of powerlessness. Thus, a belief has developed among the politically radicalized that they must dedicate themselves to changing an untenable situation.

When we asked respondents in 10 predominantly Muslim countries how they view a number of nations, the attributes they most associate with the United States are: ruthless (68%), scientifically and technologically advanced (68%), aggressive (66%), conceited (65%), and morally decadent (64%).

> *The attributes most associated with the United States are: ruthless (68%), scientifically and technologically advanced (68%), aggressive (66%), conceited (65%), and morally decadent (64%).*

The Importance of Religious and Cultural Identity

The creation of modern Muslim states after World War II brought high expectations for a strong and prosperous future. Many governments and elites looked for guidance to Western models (political, economic, legal, and education ideas and institutions). However, nation building in the Muslim world, with borders that were often drawn by European colonial powers, placed peoples with diverse, centuries-old religious, tribal, and ethnic identities and allegiances under non-elected rulers (kings, military, and ex-military). As later conflicts and civil wars in Lebanon and Iraq would demonstrate, it was a fragile process that bore the seeds for later crises of identity, legitimacy, power, and authority.

By the late 1950s and 1960s, widespread dissatisfaction with the track record of Western-inspired liberal nationalism took its toll. Monarchs and governments tumbled from power, and new rulers emerged in Egypt, Libya, Syria, Sudan, Iraq, and Algeria. All were based on some form of Arab nationalism and socialism with their populist appeals to Arab identity and unity and the promise of widespread social reforms. At the same time, Islamic movements such as the Muslim Brotherhood attracted tens of thousands of members in Egypt and Sudan as well as Syria, Jordan, and Palestine.

However, Arab nationalism and socialism were discredited by the Arab defeat in the 1967 Arab-Israeli war. Disillusionment and disenchantment were driven by a widespread feeling of

failure and loss of identity, failed political systems and economies, and the breakdown of traditional religious and social values. In response, many governments turned to Islam to buttress
their legitimacy and deal with the emergence and challenge of
Islamic reform and opposition movements. Since the 1970s,
religion and culture have remained a major force in Muslim
politics and society.

Issues of religious identity are important to both the politically
radicalized and moderates. The most frequent response to what
they admire most about themselves is "faithfulness to their religious beliefs," and the top statement they associate with Arab
and Muslim nations is: "Attachment to their spiritual and moral values is critical to their progress." But a greater emphasis on
their spiritual and moral values is what distinguishes radicals
from moderates.

In contrast to less than half (45%) the moderate group, roughly
two-thirds (65%) of the politically radicalized give top priority to holding on to their spiritual and moral values as something that is critical to their progress, and more radicals than
moderates (64% vs. 51%) say having an enriched spiritual life
is *essential*.

Responses to poll questions also reveal the belief that Muslims' Islamic heritage is in danger of being weakened by the
West's perceived denigration of Islam. Only 12% of the politically radicalized and 17% of moderates associate "respecting Islamic values" with Western nations. For both groups, the
West's "disrespect for Islam" ranks high on the list of what they

> *For politically radicalized and moderates, the West's "disrespect for Islam" ranks high on the list of what they most resent.*

most resent. Responding to an interview question on how to improve Muslim-Western relations, one 20-year-old female engineering student at the University of Jordan wrote:

> There should be rules and laws to respect people of other religions and not make fun of them. We must endeavor to relay the accurate picture of Islam to the West — showing that Islam is a religion of goodness and love, and not terrorism. The West must be willing to accept the true picture of Islam and not hold on to the negative picture that serves terrorists.[72]

Therefore, as one might expect, when asked what the Arab/Muslim world could do to improve relations with Western societies, among the top responses from moderates and the politically radicalized who offered a response is "improve the presentation of Islam to the West, present Islamic values in a positive manner."

The "War Against Islam"

Across the Muslim world from Morocco to Mindanao, the "war against Islam and Muslims" has become a popular belief and slogan. Substantial majorities in a 2007 WorldPublicOpinion.org survey of residents in Morocco, Indonesia, Egypt, and Pakistan said the United States' goal is to "weaken and divide the Islamic world."[73] Most of those surveyed see the desire to spread Christianity in the Middle East as one reason behind this goal, and to keep Islam from growing and challenging the

> *About half of both the politically radicalized and moderate groups associate "producing enjoyable films and music" with the West.*

Western way of life as another. For many, Western — and more specifically American — political, economic, military, and cultural hegemony threatens self-determination as well as Islamic identity.

Many see the allure of Western pop culture in dress, the Internet, and Western media. The Gallup World Poll found that about half of both the politically radicalized and moderate groups associate "producing enjoyable films and music" with the West. While many are attracted, many others are repulsed (not unlike many conservative Christians) because they perceive Western societies' permissiveness as an assault on Islamic values. They fear the strong appeal of Western music, movies, and TV programs, especially among the younger generation. Compounding this fear is a widespread feeling that a secular, powerful West — which does not share Muslim values — is overwhelming the Muslim world.

When Gallup asked the open-ended question: "In your own words, what do you resent most about the West?" the most frequent response across all countries among moderates and radicals is "sexual and cultural promiscuity," followed by "ethical and moral corruption" and "hatred of Muslims."

Another source of resentment stems from how Muslims are depicted in Western media. A survey of 900 film appearances of Arab characters found that the vast majority were outright racist caricatures.[74] Images of ordinary Muslims and Muslim cultures are almost nonexistent or distorted in Western mass media. Moreover, Western TV programs and films that are most popular in the Muslim world encourage a superficial emulation of Western fashions, personalities, and values.

Notably, a significantly greater proportion of the politically radicalized than moderates cite Western cultural saturation, Western immorality, and moral corruption as the top reasons for resentment. However — and this is very significant — respondents do not say, even in small percentages, that to improve relations with the Muslim world the West should "stop being immoral and corrupt." This is not at the heart of their anger. What Muslims request for better relations has nothing to do with asking people in the West to change who they are, but rather what they do: to respect Islam and Muslims and to make concrete changes in certain aspects of foreign policy. In response to a survey conducted by American University, a 16-year-old Jordanian high school student wrote:

> I believe if the West weren't stuck in their BUBBLE and actually came to this part of the world, they would see how unjustly we are treated politically (oil, Iraq, Palestine, Iran). The West needs to be better educated about this part of the world from reliable sources and form their own substantiated opinion about their ethics and not think everything Bush does is correct.[75]

Aware of international politics and committed to protecting cultural values needed for renewal and reform, the politically radicalized are far more intense in their belief that Western political, military, and cultural domination is a major threat. When asked to define their greatest fears about the future of their country, the politically radicalized frequently cite other

> *The politically radicalized (40%) are far more likely than moderates (20%) to say Western societies do not show any concern for better coexistence with the Arab-Muslim world.*

countries' interference in their internal affairs, national security, colonization, intrusion, occupation, manipulation, the fear that might is right, and U.S. dominance. In contrast, moderates most often mention economic problems.

Further illustrating this heightened intensity: The politically radicalized are far more likely than moderates to say Western societies do not show any concern for better coexistence with the Arab-Muslim world (40% vs. 20%, respectively). The politically radicalized are also far more likely than moderates to feel that the time for a better understanding between the West and the Arab/Muslim world probably will never come (37% vs. 20%, respectively).

Even more stunning, but consistent with their responses to other questions, is the extent of commitment among the politically radicalized: Fully half say that willingness to "sacrifice one's life for something one believes in" is "completely justifiable." This contrasts with only 18% of moderates who express that view.

One of the four London bombers responsible for the 7/7 terrorist attacks, Mohammad Siddique Khan, confessed his motives on a video broadcast on the al-Jazeera network:

> I and thousands like me have forsaken everything for what we believe . . . Until you stop the bombing, gassing, imprisonment and torture of my people we will not stop

this fight. We are at war and I am a soldier. Now you too will taste the reality of this situation.[76]

Although both groups are concerned about bias and Western political interference in their affairs, the greater intensity and fear that the politically radicalized express predisposes them to have a more sympathetic ear for terrorists if their grievances are not addressed. How then can these fears be addressed?

What Are the Primary Drivers of Radicalism?

A primary catalyst or driver of radicalism, often seen as inseparable from the threat to Muslim religious and cultural identity, is the threat of political domination and occupation. The interplay of the political and religious is strongly reflected in responses to open-ended questions such as: "What can the West do to improve relations with the Muslim world?" and "What is the most important thing the United States could do to improve the quality of life of people like you in this country?" Given what the politically radicalized and moderates admire about themselves and resent about the West, answers to these questions paint a consistent picture.

- Reflecting the importance of Islam, the most frequent response given by both groups to the question about what the West can do to improve relations is: more respect, consideration, and understanding of Islam as a religion; not underestimating the status of Arab/Muslim countries; being fair and less prejudiced.

- Reflecting the priority they give to democracy, the politically radicalized give equal importance to the need for political independence. Their responses include: stop interfering, meddling in our internal affairs, colonizing, and controlling natural resources.

The primacy of political grievances (Western domination and intervention) and the extent to which politics and religion have become intertwined are evident in many struggles.

The Gulf War of 1990-1991 precipitated Osama bin Laden's transformation of al-Qaeda from a support group in the Afghan-Soviet war into a global militant network. While bin Laden denounced the presence of non-Muslim armies in the homeland of Islam, Saudi Arabia, as sacrilege, he regarded the Western, especially American, military presence in Saudi Arabia as an "occupation" that would lead to increased dependency of Gulf states. More than a decade later, the U.S.-led invasion and occupation of Iraq and Israeli attacks on Gaza and Lebanon were exploited by terrorists to recruit "freedom fighters" to resist the West and protect Muslims.

The heightened sense of the West's threat to political freedom and to Islamic identity has likely reinforced the desire for *Sharia*. Recourse to *Sharia*, the blueprint for an Islamic society, provides a centuries-old paradigm. Thus, however different and diverse Muslim populations may be, for many, *Sharia* is central to faith and identity.

While moderates (83%) and political radicals (91%) alike want *Sharia* as a source of law, a significantly higher percentage of the politically radicalized (59% vs. 32% of moderates) want to see *Sharia* as the *only* source of law.

This desire for *Sharia* is reminiscent of the reasons behind the early development of Islamic law, to create a rule of law as a shield against the power of the caliph or sultan. As Richard Bulliet notes in *The Case for Islamo-Christian Civilization*: "All that restrained rulers from acting as tyrants was Islamic law, sharia. Since the law was based on divine rather than human principles, no ruler could change it to serve his own interests."[77]

Today, greater interest by the politically radicalized in the implementation of Islamic law reflects their desire to limit the power of rulers and regimes that they regard as authoritarian, "un-Islamic," and corrupt. However, this is not a call for theocracy. When asked to what extent they want religious leaders involved in public life (secular family law, curricula in schools, drafting new laws or a constitution, deciding who may run for office or how women may dress in public, or determining their country's foreign policy), majorities of the politically radicalized and moderates say they do not want religious leaders to be directly in charge. Nevertheless, radicals are more likely to want religious leaders to play an "advisory" role, consistent with the traditional role of *ulama* as "advisers" to rulers.

One of the most important insights provided by Gallup's data is that the issues that drive radicals are also issues for moderates. The critical difference between these two outlooks is one of prioritization, intensity of feeling, degree of politicization,

> *One of the most important insights provided by Gallup's data is that the issues that drive radicals are also issues for moderates.*

and alienation. This accounts for key differences in the hopes of each group.

- When asked about their dreams for the future of their country, majorities of moderates and the politically radicalized cite improved economic conditions. Greater security and an end to civil tensions are the next most frequently mentioned responses, with about one in five of the politically radicalized and moderates mentioning these.

- While moderates then focus on improvements in educational systems, the politically radicalized give higher priority to promoting democratic ideals and freedom of speech, enhancing their country's international status, earning more respect, and playing more important regional and international roles.

Is Sympathy for Terrorist Acts a Muslim Monopoly?

So far, we have discussed the percentage of respondents who sympathize with the attacks of 9/11 and what makes this fringe group of condoners different from the rest. A key question remains: If indeed Muslim sympathy for terrorism is *not* driven by religious fanaticism, then why does support for terror seemingly exist more among Muslims? Or does it? The answer is no — Muslims hold no monopoly on extremist views and are, in fact, on average more likely than the American public to unequivocally condemn attacks on civilians.

A recent study shows that only 46% of Americans think that "bombing and other attacks intentionally aimed at civilians" are "never justified," while 24% believe these attacks are "often or sometimes justified."

A recent study shows that only 46% of Americans think that "bombing and other attacks intentionally aimed at civilians" are "never justified," while 24% believe these attacks are "often or sometimes justified."[78]

Contrast this with data taken the same year from some of the largest majority Muslim nations, in which 74% of respondents in Indonesia agree that terrorist attacks are "never justified"; in Pakistan, that figure is 86%; in Bangladesh, 81%;[79] and in Iran, 80%.[80]

Similarly, 6% of the American public thinks that attacks in which civilians are targets are "completely justified." As points of comparison, in both Lebanon and Iran, this figure is 2%, and in Saudi Arabia, it's 4%. In Europe, Muslims in Paris and London are no more likely than their counterparts in the general public to believe attacks on civilians are justified and are as likely to reject violence, even for a "noble cause."

Many continue to ask: If Muslims truly reject terrorism, why does it continue to flourish in Muslim lands? What these results indicate is that terrorism is as much an "out group" activity as any other violent crime. Just as the fact that violent crimes continue to occur throughout U.S. cities does not indicate Americans' silent acquiescence to them, the continued terrorist violence is not proof that Muslims tolerate it. An abundance of statistical evidence indicates the opposite.

Diagnosis or Misdiagnosis?

Diagnosing terrorism as a symptom and Islam as the problem, though popular in some circles, is flawed and has serious risks with dangerous repercussions. It confirms radical beliefs and fears, alienates the moderate Muslim majority, and reinforces a belief that the war against global terrorism is really war against Islam. Whether one is radical or moderate, this negative attitude is a widespread perception.

In an *International Herald Tribune* op-ed piece, Fawaz Gerges recounted an interview he had with an Islamic leader in Egypt, Abed al-Rahim Barakat, who echoed the pervasive perception among Muslims that the U.S. wars in Afghanistan and Iraq are wars against Islam. "President Bush himself used the word 'crusade' to describe his war on terror," Barakat told Gerges. When Gerges responded, "It was a slip of tongue," Barakat insisted, "No, it was a Freudian slip. He revealed what he feels deep inside."[81]

Americans, like the vast majority in the Muslim world, share a fundamental aversion to extremism. Asked what they admire least about the Muslim world, Americans say overwhelmingly "extremism/radicalism/not open to others' ideas." Likewise, when asked what they admire least about their own societies, Muslims' top concerns include extremism and terrorism. This should not be surprising if we recall that the primary victims of Muslim extremism and terrorism have been Muslims. The "terrorist fringe," far from being glorified, is rejected by citizens of predominantly Muslim countries just as it is by citizens in the United States.

> *There are 1.3 billion Muslims today worldwide. If the 7% (91 million) of the politically radicalized continue to feel politically dominated, occupied, and disrespected, the West will have little, if any, chance of changing their minds.*

This amount of agreement between Muslims and Americans, plus the fact that about 9 in 10 Muslims are moderates, is the good news for those optimistic about coexistence. The bad news is the enormous gulf of perceptions between Muslims and Westerners, as well as the existence of a vast number of politically radicalized who could be pushed to support or perpetrate violence against civilians.

How wide is the gulf of perceptions? Many Muslims — both politically radicalized and moderates — say they admire the West's technology, freedom of speech, and value system of hard work. Meanwhile, as we noted earlier, Americans who were asked what they know about Muslims predominantly offer two responses: "Nothing" and "I don't know."

There are 1.3 billion Muslims today worldwide. If the 7% (91 million) of the politically radicalized continue to feel politically dominated, occupied, and disrespected, the West will have little, if any, chance of changing their minds.

KEY POINTS:

* The majority of respondents in predominantly Muslim countries condemn the events of Sept. 11, 2001.

* The minority (7%) who condone the attacks and view the United States unfavorably are no more religious than the general population.

* What does distinguish the politically radicalized from others is their perception of the West's politics, not its culture.

D R. WAFA SULTAN: *It is a clash between those who treat women like beasts, and those who treat them like human beings.*

The al-Jazeera host then asked: *I understand from your words that what is happening today is a clash between the culture of the West and the backwardness and ignorance of the Muslims?*

Dr. Wafa Sultan: *Yes, that is what I mean.*[82]

Few would be as bold as Sultan, an Arab-American psychiatrist, but many in the United States may share her view. According to a recent study sponsored by the Council on American-Islamic Relations, one of the top aspects Americans find "difficult to understand" about Islam is "oppression of women." The Gallup Poll of American households reveals similar findings where "gender inequality" is among the top responses American women give to the open-ended question: "What do you admire least about the Muslim or Islamic world?"

Statements such as Sultan's mingle with news stories of honor killings[83] in Pakistan and female genital mutilation in Somalia to cement the perception that Muslim society, and by extension, Islam, subjugates women. To many people, it therefore follows that Muslim women must want to be liberated from their faith and protected from *Sharia*, their sacred law.

The widely held perception that Muslim women are oppressed was one of the arguments used to support the invasions of both Iraq and Afghanistan. Security and liberty were imperatives — ridding the world of terror cells and those who aid them and spreading democracy and freedom, with women's rights as a centerpiece in this goal of liberation. As First Lady Laura Bush put it in a radio address delivered in November 2001: "The fight against terrorism is also a fight for the rights and dignity of women."[84]

What seems rarely to make its way into this discourse are the voices of Muslim women themselves. How do the majority of women in the Muslim world perceive Islam and their status in Muslim society? Do they feel they need to be liberated? And if so, from what and to what? Do anti-women views correlate with religiosity? Is gender as prominent an issue for them as it is for the West? What role, if any, do women want Islam to play in their daily lives and that of their societies? And perhaps most importantly, what is the best way for those concerned about Muslim women's rights to help?

Do Muslim Women Want Rights?

In the West, Muslim women have frequently been portrayed as victims of a repressive social order so severe that it renders most women in Muslim societies unaware that they even deserve rights. In 1906, a group of women missionaries held a conference on Muslim women in Cairo and published the conference proceedings in a collection called "Our Moslem Sisters: A Cry of Need from the Lands of Darkness Interpreted by Those Who Heard It."[85] The introduction reads: "They will never cry for themselves, for they are down under the yoke of centuries of oppression."

One can still hear echoes of these sentiments. In a scene in *Baby Boom*, a Hollywood movie about a high-powered career woman turned single mother, the heroine is interviewing nannies for the infant she just inherited. One of the interviewees is a woman dressed in a long black veil who speaks in a thick Arabic accent as she says, "I will teach your daughter to properly respect a man. I speak only when spoken to. I do not need a bed; I prefer to sleep on the floor." This image is reinforced by the Western press, which portrays Muslim women as silent, submissive, and relegated to the domestic sphere, while men monopolize the active roles. In a survey of all photographs of Muslims in the American press, three-quarters (73%) of the women were depicted in passive capacities, compared with less than one-sixth (15%) of the men. In photographs of the Middle East, women were six times (42%) more likely to be portrayed as victims than were men (7%).[86]

In sharp contrast to the popular image of silent submissiveness, Gallup findings on women in countries that are predominantly Muslim or have sizable Muslim populations hardly show that they have been conditioned to accept second-class status. Majorities of women in virtually every country we surveyed say that women deserve the same legal rights as men, to vote without influence from family members, to work at any job they are qualified for, and even to serve in the highest levels of government. In Saudi Arabia, for example, where as of this writing, women were not allowed to vote or drive, majorities of women say that women should be able to drive a car by themselves (61%), vote without influence (69%), and work at any job for which they are qualified (76%). Egyptian women, who have faced far fewer restrictions than their Saudi counterparts, speak even more strongly in favor of women's rights, with 88% of Egyptian women saying that they should be allowed to work at any job for which they are qualified. In Egypt, as in other parts of the Muslim world, this attitude is not just a theory, as a full third of professional and technical workers in Egypt are women, on par with Turkey and South Korea.[87]

If you want to put faces to these data, observe women such as Souad Saleh, an assertive and outspoken woman whose area of expertise is *fiqh*, or Islamic jurisprudence. Saleh is an Islamic jurist and professor at al-Azhar University, the most prominent institution of Islamic scholarship and authority in Sunni Islam. She was the first woman dean of faculty at the institution and is a prolific writer on issues ranging from family law to women's rights, authoring more than seven volumes on Islam and at least four in-depth research works. A regular on pan-Arab television and one of the most outspoken preachers on Islam, her message is clear: "Islam is simple and holds women in high esteem."[88]

Celebrity preachers aren't the only ones who defy conventional wisdom. There are also women like Salwa Riffat, an Egyptian woman now in her late 50s who earned her bachelor's degree in aeronautical engineering from Cairo University and went on to earn her Ph.D. in civil engineering. At the same time,

"Now, it's hardly something worth noting that in Egypt, universities are filled with women, in some cases more than men, and they are excelling."

she managed to successfully balance raising a family and fulfilling the demands of her career. She is now a professor of engineering, teaching men and women alike. "Women of my generation were at the forefront of a new era in Egypt," she says, referring to the wave of women attending college that gained momentum in the 1950s and 1960s. "Now, it's hardly something worth noting that in Egypt, universities are filled with women, in some cases more than men, and they are excelling." The valedictorians of Cairo's elite medical school are famously known to almost always be female.

These cases are hardly unique. Nationally representative self-reported data show percentages of women in Iran (52%), Egypt (34%), Saudi Arabia (32%), and Lebanon (37%) with post-secondary educations. In the United Arab Emirates and Iran, women make up the majority of university students. However, in Muslim countries — as well as in non-Muslim countries — Gallup finds a wide range of female education with percentages of women pursuing postsecondary educations dipping as low as 8% and 13% in Morocco and Pakistan, respectively, which is comparable with 4% in Brazil, or 11% in the Czech Republic.

Jonathan Hayden, a young American who traveled to Malaysia and Indonesia as part of a research project, met some of these female Muslim college students, who challenged a few of his own assumptions:

Some college girls approached me after a session at a University in Kuala Lumpur. After the meeting with about

100 students and teachers, I stayed behind to get a few more questionnaires. I was cornered by a group of young girls who wanted to know all about America, why we came all that way to meet them, and what our research was about. They told me about themselves and wanted to explain Islam to me. They were slightly aggressive and wanted to understand what Americans thought about them and the reasons behind some of our foreign policy decisions. But, they were also very polite and we took pictures at the end. I remember thinking at the end that this is not the picture of Muslim women that we are usually presented with in the West. They were smart, curious, and well-spoken. These were not submissive women who are forced to live a life of serving their husband. They were getting a college education and had a future that would allow them to pursue any dream that they wanted.[89]

According to the UNESCO 2005 Gender and Development report, the ratio of women to men enrolled in secondary education in 2001-2002 was 100% or higher in Jordan, Algeria, Lebanon, Kuwait, Libya, the United Arab Emirates, Indonesia, Malaysia, and Bangladesh. This compares with only 77% in Turkey, a staunchly secular nation often assumed in the West to be ahead of its neighbors in the arena of gender development, or 74% in India. The gender gap in these nations is higher than in Saudi Arabia, which boasts an 89% ratio of women to men enrolled in secondary education, according to the U.N. report.

Despite these hopeful statistics, women's basic education is still lagging in some countries. For example, in Yemen, women's literacy is only 28% versus 70% among men; in Pakistan, it is 28% versus 53% for men. These sad findings, however, are not unique to Islamic nations nor do they represent the entire Muslim world; women's literacy rates in Iran and Saudi Arabia are 70% and as high as 85% in Jordan and Malaysia.

Do Muslim Women Want to Be Liberated by the West?

The rise of the Taliban in Afghanistan in the 1990s focused the world's attention on the plight of the impoverished and war-torn country's women, who were severely restricted from education and employment. Images of silent figures draped in sky-blue *burqas* were shown, along with clips of Taliban religious police hitting a woman in the street, presumably for immodesty. Petitions, editorials, and talk shows focused on saving Afghan women from the barbaric fanaticism of their country's men. The plight of women in Afghanistan became a symbol for Muslim women in general. And the call to liberate these women, especially building up to the U.S.-led war, became a general call to save Muslim women the world over with Western values.

Some women have made this their personal cause. Among the more outspoken commentators have been Wafa Sultan, quoted at the beginning of the chapter, as well as the Somali-born former Dutch parliamentarian, Ayaan Hirsi Ali. Hirsi Ali, author of the bestseller *Infidel*, wrote in a *London Times* editorial: "I am living proof that Muslim women in the West can only benefit from turning away from the principles in their faith that justify subordination and embracing those of liberty in their host cultures."[90] Hirsi Ali's sentiment echoes 19th-century British colonialist rhetoric, such as that of Lord Cromer. The consul general of Egypt from 1883 to 1907, Cromer made the famous assertion that it was Islam's degradation of women and its insistence on veiling and seclusion that was the "fatal obstacle" to the Egyptians' "attainment of that elevation of thought and character which should accompany the introduction of Western civilization." The Egyptians should be "persuaded or forced" to become "civilized" by disposing of the veil, he claimed.

Early colonialist women in places such as Algeria also shared this attitude. Marnia Lazreg, an Algerian-born feminist scholar, analyzes this attitude toward Muslim women in her book, *The Eloquence of Silence*, where she writes:

> The veil made colonial women uncomfortable, as did every task that Algerian women performed, from rearing children to cooking and taking care of their homes. The veil, for the colonial woman, was the perfect alibi for rejecting the Algerian woman's culture and denigrating her. But it was also a constant reminder of her powerlessness in erasing the existence of a different way of being a woman. She often overcame her handicap by turning it into an advantage. She is superior to these veiled women . . .[91]

Women's perceived inferior status in Islam continues to be used as justification for cultural, and at times political, Western intervention. British parliamentarian and journalist Boris Johnson reflected this sentiment when he said in 2001: "It is time for concerted cultural imperialism. They are wrong about women. We are right."[92]

> While admiring much about the West, the majority of Muslim women do not yearn to become more like their Western counterparts. While they favor gender parity, they likely want it on their terms and within their own cultural context.

But what do the majority of Muslim women think? Gallup data concerning their perspectives toward the West are quite complex. While admiring much about the West, the majority do not yearn to become more like their Western counterparts. While they favor gender parity, they likely want it on their terms and within their own cultural context.

Consider this finding: High percentages of women and men associate "both sexes enjoy equal legal rights" with Western nations, and men and women cite political freedom, free speech, and gender equality among the most admired aspects of the West. As discussed earlier, women tell us that they believe they ought to have equal legal rights. Therefore, because Muslim women *want* legal equality and admire the West for its gender equality, we expected a high percentage to associate the statement "adopting Western values will help in their progress" with Arab and Muslim nations. However, the exact opposite turned out to be the case. For example, only 12% of Indonesian women, 20% of Iranian women, and 18% of Turkish women — who are usually assumed to be most favorable toward Westernization — associate the statement with Arab and Muslim nations.

So while expressing a positive perception of women's legal status in the West and asserting that this *should* be the case, very few respondents associate "adopting Western values will help their progress" with Muslim countries. This disconnect perplexed our researchers. Why weren't more Muslim women eager to Westernize?

A clue to this enigma came from a 22-year-old rural Moroccan woman with a secondary school education. After Gallup asked what she admires most about the West, we inquired about what she most resents. Her reply: "I resent . . . the disrespecting of women by men." Men — and in even greater percentages, women — say they resent the West's perceived promiscuity, pornography, and indecent dress — perceptions that can be traced to Hollywood images exported daily to the Muslim world. Far from inspiring an eagerness to imitate, images of scantly clad young women may leave Muslim women believing that despite Western women's equal *legal* status, their cultural status is lacking.

What makes these results even more striking is that Muslims did appear to once believe that Westernization was the way to gender equality. For example, the man dubbed the "father of Arab Feminism," Qasim Amin, contrasted "the backwardness of Muslims in the East wherever they are" with the superiority and productivity of European civilization in his 1899 book, *The Liberation of Women*.[93] Amin then proceeded to make women's liberation the catalyst for social transformation. Changing the women was necessary, Amin said, to make Muslim society abandon its backward ways and follow the Western path to success and civilization. Veiling was the most visible identity marker of the backwardness Amin sought to eradicate.

Arab intellectuals, missionaries, well-meaning European feminists, and British government officials, while disagreeing on much within their own societies, enjoyed perfect alignment in their views on what Muslim women needed: to be liberated from their backward ways to the enlightened ways of Europe, with casting off the veil as an essential first step.

The campaign to Westernize Muslim women at first seemed to work; by the 1960s, the veil could only be found among rural, peasant, or lower class urban women. Wanting to progress, the modern woman did not cover herself and looked down on those who did as old-fashioned or even backward.[94] For example, commenting on changes in her society, a 21-year-old female in Turkey writes:

> My parents did not grow up in an Islamic environment ...
> We don't care about Islamic ways. However, during my parents' time, there were people who wore the headscarf, *carsaf* (long clothing wore by women), *sarik* (clothing worn on the head by men) and I know [that] when people meet this kind of people, they always considered them to be low.[95]

Given this historical backdrop, that is likely why recent stories about increasing numbers of movie stars — long considered cultural patrons of the Western lifestyle — donning the *hijab* (headscarf) come as such a shock to so many. This same trend has been noted among the urban upper class educated women in predominantly Muslim nations as well as in the West.

Our findings are significant in that they represent an interesting adaptation of the vision set forth by Amin and his counterparts. While Westerners still often see the veil as a symbol of women's inferior status in the Muslim world, to Muslims,

> *While Westerners still often see the veil as a symbol of women's inferior status in the Muslim world, to Muslims, Western women's perceived **lack** of modesty signals their degraded cultural status in the West.*

Western women's perceived *lack* of modesty signals their degraded cultural status in the West. In both cases, the assumption is that women are either covering or uncovering to please or obey men. For example, a woman that Gallup interviewed in Malaysia says she feels sorry for women in the West because they don't love themselves enough and feel they must give in to men's sexual desires.

Other polls in the Middle East and Asia also show that majorities of Muslims in Egypt, Jordan, and Pakistan do not believe that women are respected in Western societies.[96] The data simply do not support the persistent popular perception in the West that Muslim women can't wait to be liberated from their culture and adopt the ways of the West.

So are Muslim women pro-West or anti-West? The answer is more complex than the question. While Muslim women admire much about the West, they do not favor a wholesale cultural transplant. Two attributes that many of those surveyed associate with their societies reflect this nuanced perspective: "eager to have better relationship with the Western world" and "attachment to their spiritual and moral values is critical to their progress."

This dual message was what Frankie Martin, an American college student, heard during his travels to Jordan, Pakistan, and India. As a part of his research project, he visited a *Sharia* class at the University of Jordan:

The men remained rather quiet, asking a few questions but with a reserved tone. It was the women, all of whom wore the *hijab* in some form, who asked the tough questions, again running against my expectations. I received many questions from the women, ranging from the U.S. wars in Iraq and Afghanistan to support for Israel to the Danish cartoon controversy and perceptions of Islam in America. They asked their questions with a kind of intensity I had never experienced. In response to their questions, I told the young women that I was in their country to listen, a college student just like they were, and that they should speak away. I saw deep frustrations bubbling to the surface. For many, I was the first American they had the opportunity to have a discussion with and they wanted me to know what they were going through. They wanted me to feel what they were feeling. They were not rude, just assertive, and while the men sat on the sidelines, the women asked questions that even bordered on the mischievous and feisty: "If you like Islam so much why don't you convert?" or reflected serious concerns like, "Why in America are all Muslims seen as terrorists?"

The women didn't just sit and listen, they engaged, and responded to comments I made. When I told them that I believed Islam was a religion of peace with a core of compassion and tolerance, one female college student stopped me. "Islam is peaceful but it is also proud, strong, and just," she told me in a somewhat warning tone, concerned I was making her religion too "soft." These girls were sick of being humiliated, not as women in an oppressive Islamic society, as a Westerner might think, but as Muslims at

the hands of perceived
Western aggression and
misunderstanding.

*Polling data from Iraq illustrate
the gap between anecdotal
portrayals of Muslim women's
sentiment and actual sentiment
measured by representative
survey data.*

Despite their anger and resentment toward the U.S. administration, they stressed to me that they wanted to reach out to the U.S., but wanted the Americans to also reach out to them and understand what they were going through. They sought to foster greater dialogue and understanding between Islam and the West. Although they seemed to despise U.S. foreign policy, they took pains to explain that they didn't have a problem with me — or other Americans for that matter.[97]

How Do Muslim Women Feel About Islam and Its Sacred Law?

Iraqi Governing Council ... ordering in late December that family laws shall be "canceled" and such issues placed under the jurisdiction of strict Islamic legal doctrine known as Sharia.

This week, outraged Iraqi women — from judges to cabinet ministers — denounced the decision in street protests and at conferences.

The Washington Post
Jan. 15, 2004

Polling data from Iraq collected after the Governing Council's vote[98] illustrate the gap between anecdotal portrayals of Muslim women's sentiment and actual sentiment measured by representative survey data. The seemingly authoritative *Washington*

Post article does not cover the opinion of a single woman who supported placing family law under the *Sharia* in Iraq's constitution. Yet 58% of Iraqi women were found to *oppose* separation of religion from political power, and 81% said religious authorities should play a direct role in crafting family law.

Are Muslim women, who are relatively well-educated and aware of their deserved rights, hostile toward Islam? Not according to our data. One of the most pronounced themes to emerge from our study of the Muslim world was the great importance of faith in respondents' personal lives and in society. Substantial majorities in virtually all predominantly or substantially Muslim countries Gallup surveyed say "religion is an important part of life." And as stated earlier, the aspect most frequently associated with Muslim societies, on average, is "attachment to their spiritual and moral values is critical to their progress." When asked what they most admire about their own societies, by far, the most frequent response to this open-ended question is "faithful/sincere/attached to religious beliefs/adhere or respect teachings of Islam."

There was no systemic gender difference in the responses. Like their male counterparts, women overwhelmingly say that their faith is personally important as well as their society's greatest asset. In some countries, such as Egypt, Morocco, and Jordan, a significantly higher percentage of women than men cite people's faith as their most admired aspect of the Muslim world.

The book *Politics of Piety: The Islamic Revival and the Feminist Subject* discusses Hajja Samira, a woman who leads a religious study group in a mosque situated in one of Cairo's middle-class suburbs. Samira represents a growing movement of women who are working to revive what they believe is their society's greatest asset: Islam. "Our sight, dress, drink, and food should be for God and out of love for him," she says. "They will tell you this way of life is uncivilized: Don't listen to them because you know that real civilization for we Muslims is closeness to God."[99]

Hajja Faiza, another leader in the same informal movement, explains how she is working to bring Islam back into her society's daily life — to turn it from mere ritual to a living reality in the way people interact:

> The challenge that we face as Muslims right now is how to understand and follow the example of the Prophet, how to act in accord with the Quran and the *hadith* in our daily lives. All of us know the basics of religion, such as praying, fasting, and other acts of worship. But the difficult question that confronts us today as Muslims is how to make our daily lives congruent with our religion, while at the same time moving with the world.[100]

Faiza's desire to see Islam as more than a private ritual is not unique. Majorities of women in nearly all majority Muslim nations surveyed say that *Sharia* should at least be *a* source of legislation. In addition, most women say that religion plays an important role in their personal lives. At the same time, majorities assert their rights to the ballot, in the workplace, and to serve in the highest levels of government. Muslim women do not regard Islam as an obstacle to their progress; indeed, many may see it as a crucial component of that progress.

*Working for women's progress by drawing upon the **Sharia** instead of by eliminating it is a re-emerging theme among contemporary Muslim societies.*

Working for women's progress by drawing upon the *Sharia* instead of by eliminating it is a re-emerging theme among contemporary Muslim societies. For example, when a special committee made up of representatives from the Mecca Governorate, the Presidency of the Two Holy Mosques Affairs, and the King Fahd Institute for Hajj Research proposed shifting the present prayer area for women from the *mataf* (circumambulation area) to two other locations on the ground floor on the northern side of the Grand Mosque, women protested using religious arguments. The officials' argument was that the new arrangement would allow women to get a larger prayer space in the new area and that they'd be safe from overcrowding and away from the glare of television cameras.[101] The women who successfully mobilized against this proposal did so not by depending on secular arguments or international pressure from human rights organizations, but instead by arguing that it was against the Islamic tradition.

"Banning women from praying at the *Kaaba* esplanade is unprecedented in the Islamic history," wrote female historian and author Hatoon al-Fassi.[102] "Both sexes are equal when it comes to performing their religious duties and in terms of rewards and punishments. The Prophet (peace be upon him) has instructed that women must not be banned from mosques," al-Fassi argued.[103] She ended her appeal by saying, "I am sure they will not accept the panel's proposal, which violates the spirit and message of Islam that was sent for all of humanity without any discrimination."[104]

Suhaila Hammad, a female Saudi member of a body of world Muslim scholars, argued that the proposal was discriminatory and therefore religiously unacceptable. "Both men and women have the right to pray in the House of God. Men have no right to take it away," she said.[105]

Asifa Quraishi, a law professor at the University of Wisconsin and an advocate for women's rights, argues that the most effective means to oppose practices done in the name of *Sharia* that are hurtful to women is to challenge the compliance of these laws to Islamic principles, instead of arguing for the removal of *Sharia*. For example, Pakistan's rape laws have understandably come under heavy attack from human rights organizations. The way the law is written, a rape victim requires four adult male eyewitnesses to the assault to prosecute her attacker. Not only that, but if the victim becomes pregnant as a result of the attack, she could face fornication charges while her attacker could walk away free.

Attacks on these laws usually take the form of attacking *Sharia* itself. This approach elicits a defensive response from a country in which a majority wants Islamic religious principles to be the only source of legislation. Instead of attacking *Sharia*, Quraishi challenges the very assumption that this law is *Sharia*-compliant. Through her Islamic critique, using the Quran and prophetic tradition, Quraishi argues that the laws actually violate *Sharia* and should be repealed for this reason.[106] Women's rights advocates in Pakistan have used arguments like Quraishi's to challenge Pakistan's discriminatory rape laws. In November 2006, Pakistan's parliament amended the 1979 rape laws with the passage of the Women's Protection Bill.[107]

> *The World Health Organization estimates that female circumcision affects 100 million to 140 million girls and women a year.*

These cases involved initiatives led by Muslim women, but there are also examples of concerned Western advocates successfully working within an Islamic framework to bring about positive change. In 2000, Rüdiger Nehberg, a German man, founded TARGET, a human rights organization dedicated to fighting female genital mutilation. He approached the problem as one that *violates* Islamic principles, not one caused by Islam.

The World Health Organization estimates that the practice, sometimes also called female circumcision, affects 100 million to 140 million girls and women a year, both inside and outside predominantly Muslim societies. According to the United Nations Children's Fund (UNICEF), at least 90% of all women are circumcised in Egypt, Mali, Guinea, and Sudan, while almost no women are circumcised in Iraq, Iran, and Saudi Arabia.[108] Wherever Nehberg goes, he says that "this custom can only be brought to an end with the power of Islam." In December 2006, a conference of high-ranking Muslim theologians, hosted by the Egyptian Grand Mufti Ali Gomaa, and attended by the prominent Egyptian scholar Yusuf al-Qaradawi, agreed that the practice of female genital mutilation is irreconcilable with Islam.[109]

Using *Sharia* arguments to oppose unjust practices is not a completely new phenomenon. For example, a famous incident from early Muslim history shows that women challenged even the highest political and religious authorities using arguments from the Quran. When Omar ibn al-Khattab, Sunni Islam's second caliph, proposed a cap on the amount women could stipulate for their *mahr*, a gift given to the bride by her husband upon marriage, a woman objected. She publicly questioned Omar, "How can you limit what God has not?" and went on to cite the Quranic verse guaranteeing a woman's right to receive her *mahr* in full. Omar then realized his mistake and rescinded his proposal.

A Different Way of Understanding Equality: Do the "Same" Legal Rights Always Mean Fairness to Women?

While Egyptian women agree that women should vote for whomever they wish without interference (95%) and work at any job they are qualified to fill (88%), their enthusiasm for "the same legal rights" is more muted (69%). A similar pattern is found among women in Jordan, where a significant percentage (30%), though still a minority, disagree that women and men should have the *same* legal rights, although they agree that women should have rights to the ballot and the workplace.

Interestingly, the women who disagree with giving women the "same" legal rights as men are not less educated than their counterparts. They are, however, more likely to favor *Sharia* as the only source for legislation. So do women who support *Sharia* oppose gender equality? Not necessarily. Rather, some Muslim women believe that having *the same* legal rights does not always mean fair and just treatment of women, because men and women have different roles in a family. In the words of one Egyptian woman: "Giving a farmer and a carpenter both a hammer as a tool to help their work is certainly treating them the *same*, but not *fairly*."

One example from Islamic jurisprudence may help to explain what she means: Men and women have the same legal rights in matters of crime and punishment, financial interactions, and other matters of civic law. However, in Muslim family law, the area of *Sharia* most strongly criticized in the West for gender discrimination, men and women share different, "complementary" rights — ones that do not necessarily favor men. For example, according to a unanimous opinion of Muslim jurists, a woman carries no financial obligation for the family. She maintains the right to keep her earned wages and property under her name alone, instead of as "communal property." However, she and her children have legal rights to her husband's property and earnings. Men are also financially responsible for wedding expenses, housing, and the *mahr*.

Even if she is very wealthy, a woman is never financially responsible for supporting anyone, not even herself. The "complement" to this financial advantage is that her inheritance is a 1:2 ratio to that of her brother's. The rationale for this law is that while a woman may work, she should never be *obligated* to work. And therefore, her closest male relative is responsible for her financial support. Because her financial responsibility is zero, in theory, and her brother is responsible for his own family and potentially for his mother and other female siblings if they are not married, giving his sister a third of the inheritance may seem unfairly generous to some. Giving women the "same" legal rights as men would obviously do away with this advantage that Muslim women have historically enjoyed.

How Do Muslim Women Feel About the Muslim World?

*Although Muslim women value the role Islam plays in their personal lives and favor a role for **Sharia** as at least an aspect of their public lives, they are not uncritical of the Muslim world.*

Although Muslim women value the role Islam plays in their personal lives and favor a role for *Sharia* as at least an aspect of their public lives, they are not uncritical of the Muslim world. What women say they admire least about Arab/Muslim societies is similar to what their male counterparts complain about: lack of unity, economic and political corruption, and extremism.

As Marina Ottaway of the Carnegie Endowment for International Peace points out, Muslim women are operating in a larger context of limited political freedom, economic deterioration, and global injustice — problems that confront all citizens of the Muslim world.[110] Considering the political stagnation and democracy deficit in many of these countries, it is not surprising that gender inequality did not generate the frequency of spontaneous responses one might expect to this open-ended question. In Gallup's surveys, gender inequality is not mentioned at all in Jordan and mentioned by only 1% of women in Egypt and 2% in Morocco. It is mentioned by 5% of women in Saudi Arabia, but it is outranked by "lack of unity" and "high unemployment."

Overall, Muslim women favor Islam's role in their lives, but they see a gap between the ideal and the Muslim world's reality. Hajja Samira summarizes this sentiment well in her critique of modern Muslim society: "We are Muslim in name, but our acts are not those of Muslims."[111]

In Saudi Arabia, the majority of men (58%) say they believe women should vote, a startlingly high endorsement of an illegal act.

How Do Muslim *Men* Feel About Women's Rights?

Another issue worth examining is whether men in the Muslim world believe that women should have rights. The short answer is yes, they do. But in some countries, men respond with less enthusiasm than do the women. For example, in Morocco, 97% of women, versus 72% of men, say the government should guarantee a woman's right to vote without interference from her family. However, the gender gap is less significant in Iran, often assumed to be home to repressive male attitudes toward women, where 87% of men and 91% of women believe that women should be allowed to vote. Iranian women gained suffrage in the White Revolution in 1963. In Saudi Arabia, where women do not yet have the right to vote, the majority of men (58%) say they believe women should vote, a startlingly high endorsement of an illegal act. In several countries, such as Indonesia, Malaysia, Turkey, and Lebanon, there was no observable gender gap in response to this question.

Majorities of men in virtually every country surveyed, including 62% in Saudi Arabia, 73% in Iran, and 81% in Indonesia, also agree that women should be allowed to work at any job for which they are qualified.

Amr Khaled, by far the most popular religious preacher in the Arab world and one of *Time* magazine's 100 most influential people in the world in 2007, in many ways represents Arab men's (and women's) growing recognition of gender equity as consistent with Islam and not a Western import. Khaled, a young Egyptian accountant turned religious teacher who sports tailored suits instead of the robes of the *mullahs*, teaches that women's status in Islam is not only "equal" to men, but that women carry a special gift. "God created women as a mercy to the world," he tells the millions who watch his television program on *Iqra'* (Read), an Arabic satellite channel devoted to religious programming. "Women's status in Islam is unmatched by any other system," he says, "but we Muslims have ignored these rights for too long."

Khaled emphasizes that men and women must balance their family obligations and their public roles as builders of their communities and countries. His message of women's respected place in Islam is attractive to millions across the Arab world as well as among Muslims in the West.

Despite these developments, there are still significant gender gaps in attitudes toward women's rights. In Saudi Arabia, for example, a slight majority of men (55%) say that women should not be allowed to drive a car by themselves, whereas only 34% of Saudi women agree, representing the largest gender gap observed on this question. Gaps in the percentage of men versus women who favor women's rights in some parts of the Muslim world signal that significant work remains to be done to bring about a shared vision regarding women's role in society.

Is Islam the Problem?

Because anti-women views are often believed to result from religious sentiment, important questions that must be asked

*Is there merit to the arguments
of those who say that women's
lagging status in much of the
Muslim world is attributable to
Islamic principles?*

are: Does religiosity among
Muslim men correlate with
less egalitarian views toward
women? Is there merit to the arguments of those who say that
women's lagging status in much of the Muslim world is attributable to Islamic principles?

Our data analysis would say no to both questions. When we
compared the men who say that women and men should have
the same legal rights with men who espouse the opposite view,
for the most part, we found little difference in their degree of
religiosity. In fact, in Lebanon, Morocco, and Iran, men who
support women's rights are found to be more religious than
those who do not support women's rights. The only exception
among the eight countries[112] included in this analysis is Turkey,
where the opposite is true. In Turkey, in contrast to other parts
of the Muslim world, religiosity correlates heavily with *lack* of
education, which could explain this result.

A similar trend is evident among men convicted of honor
killings, long believed to be the result of religious zeal. For
example, research indicates that 69.4% of the men who
committed honor killings in Jordan did not perform their daily
prayers, and 55.5% did not fast.[113] That these men fail to observe
the most obligatory rituals of Islam suggests that their act of
murder is not motivated by religious zeal or devotion. Rather,
other factors normally associated with criminal behavior are
more likely to play a role. For example, most of these men had a
record of violent behavior: 35.1% had already served sentences
for previous crimes. Furthermore, 32.4% were illiterate, only

3.7% had attended college, and 24.1% were brought up in broken homes.[114]

The Challenge

During her listening tour of Egypt, Saudi Arabia, and Turkey in September 2005, Karen Hughes, the undersecretary of public diplomacy, encountered the huge obstacles that well-meaning Western women face in their efforts to help Muslim women.

During her stop in Saudi Arabia, Hughes encountered Arab pride at a meeting with Saudi women college students and faculty at a women's university in the coastal city of Jeddah. Hughes compared the status of Saudi women to the "broken wing" of a bird because they lack the right of full participation, including the rights to vote and drive.[115] Her assertion was met with indignation. Students and teachers expressed their frustration at the stereotype of Saudi women as oppressed and blasted the U.S. media for promoting such an image. "I think I speak for all of us, and we're happy. We're not only content, we're happy. So what steps are you taking to show that image?" one woman objected.

But Gallup data show that the majority of Saudi women say that they should have the right to vote and to drive. So why the negative reaction to Hughes' assertion?

In Saudi Arabia, Hughes came face-to-face with the Saudi perception that the United States feels culturally superior to Muslims and believes itself to be in a position to "save them"

> *When pressed by Western reporters, some women conceded that they would like to drive and vote, but insisted that change would come at Saudi Arabia's pace and choosing.*

with little regard for their culture and values. This is partly why Saudi women reacted defensively to her speech, as have other Arab women when confronted with the perceived threat of cultural domination. When pressed by Western reporters after the function, some women conceded that they would like to drive and vote, but insisted that change would come at Saudi Arabia's pace and choosing.[116]

In Turkey, acute conflicts such as the war in neighboring Iraq, which has hurt many women, made Hughes' claim that she cared about women lead to accusations of hypocrisy from even Westernized Turkish feminists. In Egypt, anger at perceived U.S. opposition to genuine Arab political autonomy made even an educated, cosmopolitan, and democratically minded Egyptian woman like Amani Fikri, an editor at an opposition newspaper, question Hughes' motives and sincerity.

These three dimensions — perceived cultural disrespect, perception of political domination, and the reality of acute conflicts — are the filters through which many Muslim men and women view Western — especially American — actions and words. Each filter reinforces and is reinforced by the other, and each dimension is seen through the filter of the other two. For example, Rushdi, a mini-van driver in Cairo, said, "America hates Islam; look at what they did to Iraq." In this case, the acute conflict is seen through the filter of perceived U.S. hatred for Islam, and in turn, is reinforced by it.

Should Westerners simply apply "cultural relativism" and regard women's suffering in a "non-judgmental" manner?

Ironically, all three dimensions are at least partly related to Muslim women's rights — a major complicating factor. Western attacks on Islam often use women's rights as a justification. Also, as discussed before, acute conflicts such as the invasions of Afghanistan and Iraq were both partially justified in the name of the liberation of women. Yet, Muslims believe that these wars have harmed rather than helped Muslim lands. Muslim men and women alike believe that the invasion of Iraq has done a great deal more harm than good — this is the sentiment of majorities in most of the countries in which this question was asked.[117] Add to this Muslims' perception that Western concern for Muslim women is limited to the abuse they might suffer at the hands of Muslim men, while the suffering that women endure at the hands of Western powers appears to be ignored.

Moreover, those who argue against free elections in many parts of the Muslim world use the fear that elections will produce anti-women Islamic fundamentalists as justification. However, especially in countries where this argument is made the strongest, such as Egypt, women in majorities say democracy will help their country's progress and that they favor *Sharia* as a source of legislation.

Where to Go From Here?

Do these sentiments mean that Westerners should simply apply "cultural relativism" and regard women's suffering in a "non-judgmental" manner? Should they stand quietly on the sidelines and mind their own business? Not at all. But the mix of perception, history, and current reality presents a serious challenge for even the most well-meaning Western advocate for Muslim women and therefore demands that they proceed with caution, consistency, and respect. Our analysis yields the following recommendations.

Put First Things First

Before Westerners can help Muslim women, they must understand Muslim women's priorities. Professor Azizah al-Hibri, a Lebanese-American law professor at the University of Richmond and founder of KARAMAH, an organization of female Muslim lawyers dedicated to defending women's human rights, explains the frustration of "Third World" women at what they see as a dictation from "First World" women as to what their priorities need to be, especially at international conferences on human rights:

> In Copenhagen, Third World women were told that their highest priorities related to the veil and clitoridectomy (female genital mutilation). In Cairo, they were told that their highest priorities related to contraception and abortion. In both cases, Third World women begged to differ. They repeatedly announced that their highest priorities were peace and development. They noted that they could not very well worry about other matters when their children were dying from thirst, hunger or war.[118]

Muslim women, like Muslim men, say that their most pressing issues include economic development and political reform. Thus, the challenges to greater equality and fuller female political participation cannot be overcome without addressing the more serious problem of authoritarianism in much of the

> *Democratization is not a byproduct of female empowerment; rather, it is a criterion for it.*

Muslim world. While the United States has made the issue of women a primary focus in its Middle East foreign policy, it is equally important to exert as much effort and attention to the promotion of democracy, because the former cannot be divorced from the latter. There can be no real democracy in the Muslim world that does not recognize and include women as full and equal participants in all spheres of life. Democracy needs women in order to be an inclusive, representative, and enduring system of government, so it is critical to recognize that democratization is not a byproduct of female empowerment; rather, it is a criterion for it.

The same can be said about economic development. According to Ronald Inglehart, who has studied global values for decades through the World Values Survey, human development in almost any society begins with economic modernization and development, which in turn demands the integration of women into the workplace, which in turn brings about cultural change, not the other way around.[119] Some have argued that economic stagnation, especially in the Arab world, is attributable to underutilization of women as a human resource because of traditional cultural values.[120] However, with high Arab male unemployment rates, the issue does not seem to be a lack of use of human resources, but rather low demand for these resources because of a shortage of economic opportunity in general.

There is certainly a need to improve women's status globally, but focusing primarily on gender issues in the Arab world while dismissing more basic needs such as stability, economic improvement, and political rights ignores not only the natural sequence of societal development, but more importantly, the stated priorities of Muslim women themselves. Their priorities, not those of their advocates, should be the guidepost for any advocacy that has Muslim women's interests at heart.

Show Consistency of Concern

Lila Abu-Lughod, a professor of anthropology and women's and gender studies at Columbia University and a staunch defender of women's rights who has worked on women's issues in the Middle East for 20 years, writes why she was uncomfortable when asked to sign a petition to save Afghan women from the Taliban. She notes:

> I had never received a petition from such women defending the right of Palestinian women to safety from Israeli bombing or daily harassment at check-points. Maybe some of these same people might be signing petitions to save African women from genital cutting, or Indian women from dowry deaths. However, I do not think that it would be as easy to mobilize so many of these American and European women if it were not a case of Muslim men oppressing Muslim women — women ... for whom they can feel sorry and in relation to whom they can feel smugly superior.[121]

This perception can be altered by making Western advocacy for "women's rights" more consistent within the greater context of human rights, including harm caused by poverty, political repression, and war — especially when Western policies are perceived to have caused these hardships.

Move Beyond Feminism vs. Fundamentalism

According to Asifa Quraishi, during the 1993 United Nations population conference in Cairo, there was a strong push by Western feminists on the issue of abortion, framing the matter as a woman's right versus the oppressive limitations of religious law. The irony is that Islamic law contains differing opinions as to abortion's permissibility, and its approach is more ambiguous and nuanced than, say, the Catholic Church's strictures against the procedure. However, this framing and the strong push led Egypt's senior religious leader, the Sheikh of al-Azhar, to issue an opinion definitively against abortion, making it harder for women to safely obtain the procedure than it was previously. Quraishi sees basic misconceptions about Islam and Islamic law as the main causes of these unintended negative consequences and argues that Western feminists sometimes have an "innate, often subconscious sense of superiority" and approach issues facing Muslim women with a "rescue mentality."[122]

This example, and many like it, illustrate the strategic danger of approaching women's rights in the Muslim world as a struggle between Islam and Western egalitarian values. It leaves women and their supporters with no options, and it empowers those who oppose rights for women in the name of resistance to Western hegemony. Muslim women see no contradiction between the faith they cherish and the rights they deserve. Far from being an obstacle to progress, Islam is seen as a crucial part of this progress. Hence, any solution toward greater gender justice should use, not eliminate, indigenous cultural and religious frameworks that grant women the rights they desire.

Fatima Gailani, a U.S.-based adviser to one of the female dele-
gations at a Bonn peace conference discussing the rebuilding of
Afghanistan, said, "If I go to Afghanistan today and ask women
for votes on the promise to bring them secularism, they are going to tell me to go to hell."[123] She is probably right. Only 5%
of Afghan women say *Sharia* should have no role in forming
legislation, whereas 85% say it should be at least a source of
legislation (45% say it should be the only source).

Therefore, reform in Muslim societies will likely be most effective if promoted within an Islamic framework. This was the
case when women objected to the proposal to bar women from
praying in the central portion of the Grand Mosque in Mecca;
and when Muslim scholars issued a statement against female
genital mutilation in light of Islamic teachings; and when Pakistani women used Quranic teachings to amend the discriminatory rape laws.

The first step in helping Muslim women improve their situation is to question the assumption that religious teachings are
the root cause of women's societal struggles. We do so by understanding the tradition of gender justice in Islam and gaining
an appreciation for the nuances of Islamic law and the diversity
of internal debates within Islam.

Decouple Libertinism from Liberation
Vida Samadzai appeared in 2003 at the Miss Earth beauty pageant in Manila representing Afghanistan. Unlike the other con-
testants, she was not nominated by her country, but instead was
"appointed" by people who were aware of her volunteer work.

Afghanistan's minister for women's affairs, in a strong statement, said Samadzai did not represent Afghan women or their plight for freedom. "Appearing naked before a camera or television is not women's freedom but in my opinion is to entertain men," said then-minister Habiba Surabi. "We condemn Vida Samadzai, she is not representing Afghanistan's women, and this is not women's freedom," she asserted. Surabi went on to say that in Afghan culture, a woman's worth should not be measured by her "beauty" or body but by her skills and knowledge.

Samadzai herself conceded that she was uncomfortable about being required to wear the two-piece bikini. "I know that . . . it's caused a lot of controversy and I didn't feel comfortable wearing it . . . because it's not just my culture," said Samadzai.[124]

Though Samadzai's appearance at the pageant in a bikini was neither sanctioned by Afghanistan nor seen by its minister for women's affairs as a forward step for women's rights, nor even something with which Samadzai herself felt entirely comfortable, some Western observers said it was a sign of progress for women in Afghanistan and everywhere. Judges at the Miss Earth beauty pageant announced that, for the first time, they were handing out a "beauty for a cause" prize. They awarded it to Samadzai for "symbolizing the newfound confidence, courage and spirit of today's women" and "representing the victory of women's rights and various social, personal and religious struggles."

If we associate women's rights with aspects of the West that Muslim women and men alike resent, we will embolden those for whom opposition to women's rights is a bulwark against

> *Conflating libertinism with liberation only empowers critics and weakens those who wish to make positive change for women from within.*

Western hegemony. Indeed, those who oppose more egalitarian interpretations of Islam do so in the name of "cultural preservation" against the perceived onslaught of morally corrupting Western influence. Conflating libertinism with liberation only empowers these critics and weakens those who wish to make positive change for women from within.

KEY POINTS:

* Muslim women cherish their religion *and* their rights.

* While Muslim women admire aspects of the West, they do not endorse wholesale adoption of Western values.

* Majorities of Muslim women believe that their most urgent needs are not gender issues, but greater political and economic development.

* Western advocacy of women's issues is often eyed suspiciously because feminism was used historically to justify colonialism.

Chapter 5: **Clash or Coexistence?**

O
UR WORLD ISN'T SAFER; it's more dangerous. A major source of that danger, global terrorism, is on the rise and will likely remain a threat for the foreseeable future. The data from our worldwide poll offer serious challenges to many predominant beliefs affecting our perspectives and policies. Critical to the fight against global terrorism is an ability to move beyond presuppositions and stereotypes in our attitudes and policies and to form partnerships that transcend an "us" and "them" view of the world.

Myths vs. Realities

Myth: Muslims Are the Culprits
On December 7, 2004, Kofi Annan, then-Secretary General of the United Nations, convened a U.N. conference, "Confronting Islamophobia: Education for Tolerance and Understanding," at which he noted:

> [When] the world is compelled to coin a new term to take account of increasingly widespread bigotry — it is a sad and troubling development. Such is the case with "Islamo-phobia." . . . Since the September 11 attacks on the United States, many Muslims, particularly in the West, have found themselves the objects of suspicion, harassment and dis-crimination. . . . Too many people see Islam as a monolith

*Blaming Islam is a simple
answer, easier and less
controversial than re-examining
the core political issues and
grievances that resonate in much
of the Muslim world.*

and as intrinsically op-
posed to the West . . .
[The] caricature remains
widespread and the gulf of
ignorance is dangerously deep.[125]

We live in a world in which two of the great world religions
with Semitic origins are often under siege. For discrimination
and prejudice against the world's 14 million Jews, we have a
powerful term, *anti-Semitism*.[126] Until recently, no comparable
term has existed for prejudice, discrimination, and violence directed toward the 1.3 billion Muslims in the world. The term
Islamophobia was coined to describe a two-stranded form of
racism — rooted in both the "different" physical appearance
of Muslims and also in an intolerance of their religious and
cultural beliefs.[127]

The catastrophic events of 9/11 and continued terrorist attacks
in Muslim countries and in Madrid and London have exacerbated the growth of Islamophobia almost exponentially. Islam
and Muslims have become guilty until proven innocent. The religion of Islam is regarded as the cause, rather than the context,
for radicalism, extremism, and terrorism.

But blaming Islam is a simple answer, easier and less controversial than re-examining the core political issues and grievances that resonate in much of the Muslim world: the failures
of many Muslim governments and societies, some aspects of
U.S. foreign policy representing intervention and dominance,
Western support for authoritarian regimes, the invasion and

occupation of Iraq, or support for Israel's military battles with Hamas in Gaza and Hezbollah in Lebanon.

Prominent leaders of the Christian Right in the United States have been quick to demonize Islam. On NBC News in late 2001, Franklin Graham, the Rev. Billy Graham's son and successor, declared Islam a "very evil and very wicked religion." On Fox News' *Hannity & Colmes* in September 2002, televangelist and founder of the Christian Coalition, the Rev. Pat Robertson, called the Prophet Muhammad "an absolute wild-eyed fanatic . . . a robber and brigand . . . a killer" and declared that "to think that [Islam] is a peaceful religion is fraudulent." The late Jerry Falwell, appearing on CBS' *60 Minutes* in 2002 called the Prophet Muhammad "a terrorist."

Not all evangelical leaders, however, share this view of Islam. Dr. Richard Land, the president of the Ethics & Religious Liberty Commission at the Southern Baptist Convention, condemned these statements by fellow evangelicals. "I disagree with those statements, as do many evangelicals. You know, one of the definitions of a leader is they have followers, and some of the people you've mentioned have fewer followers each year," he said. "I thought that they [the statements] were erroneous and wrong." But Land's statements did not receive wide media attention.[128]

Anti-Muslim sentiments aren't limited to some prominent Christians; they are fairly common among political commentators too. One such commentator, Daniel Pipes, referring to the capture of a sniper in the Washington, D.C., area claimed:

It came as no surprise to learn that the lead suspect as the Washington, D.C.-area sniper is John Allen Muhammad, an African-American who converted to Islam about 17 years ago. Nor that seven years ago he provided security for Louis Farrakhan's "Million Man March." . . . All this was near-predictable because it fits into a well-established tradition of American blacks who convert to Islam turning against their country. Of course, this is not a universal pattern, as some of the roughly 700,000 African-American converts to Islam are moderate and patriotic citizens.[129]

Myth: Europe's Future Is "Eurabia"

Islamophobia has taken an even more alarmist turn in the charge that Europe is in danger of becoming Islamized and transformed into a new Muslim stronghold, Eurabia. This fear is based on the presumption that Islam is hostile to, and incompatible with, Western values. It presumes that the growth of Muslim populations in Europe will eventually result in a Muslim demographic majority, which will threaten the historically Christian and now overwhelmingly secular nature of European society.

Fear of Eurabia is reflected and reinforced by statements like that of prominent Princeton historian Bernard Lewis, who declared in the German daily *Die Welt* in 2004 and again in a more expanded form in the *Jerusalem Post* in 2007 that Europe would be Islamic by the end of this century "at the very latest." In 2004, Frits Bolkestein of the Netherlands, an outgoing European Union commissioner, warned that immigration was turning the EU into "an Austro-Hungarian empire on a grand scale." He alluded to great cities that would soon be minority-European — two of which, Amsterdam and Rotterdam, are in his own country — and warned that the (projected) addition of 83 million Muslim Turks would further the Islamization of Europe. Bolkestein commented that he did not know whether things would turn out as Lewis predicted. "But if he *is* right," Bolkestein added, "the liberation of Vienna [from Turkish armies] in 1683 will have been in vain."[130]

Jean-Marie Le Pen, the president of France's far-right National Front party, speaking of Muslims, said:

> These elements have a negative effect on all of public security. They are strengthened demographically both by natural reproduction and by immigration, which reinforces their stubborn ethnic segregation, their domineering nature. This is the world of Islam in all its aberrations.[131]

Norway's right-wing Kristiansand Progress party claimed that Hitler's *Mein Kampf* and the Quran were one and the same and wanted Islam banned in Norway.[132] In Denmark, Islamophobic attitudes and behavior, and negative stereotypes in media, led to an outbreak of verbal and physical abuse and attacks (arson, bombs, graffiti) against individuals, religious centers, and commercial properties. Danish Muslims were called upon to affirm that the Danish constitution was above the Quran.[133]

Is Eurabia really a significant threat? Here again, the tendency to see Muslims as a monolithic block and other myths are trumped by reality. The heart of the myth and fear of Eurabia has to do with Muslim demographics, the potency of Islam in Europe, and the attacks and thwarted attacks of militants in London, Madrid, and other European cities. But in reality, only 4% (20 million) of the European Union's population is Muslim. Even if Turkey were admitted to the European Union, something that is not likely in the near future (and, some would argue, not likely ever), that would raise the percentage of Muslims to 17%. Most importantly, like other religious and ethnic groups, Europe's Muslims are not homogenous. They represent diverse ethnic groups that often have little in common: South Asians in Britain, North Africans in France, and Turks in Germany. Moreover, many do not even practice their religion. They are at best cultural Muslims. Indeed, most of those who rioted and torched France's *banlieues* (suburbs) in 2005 were not mosquegoers.

Myth: "They Hate Us Because of Our Freedom . . ."

What we in the West think of Muslims and Islam is crucial to the formulation and the success or failure of our policies and of relations with much of the Muslim world. The conventional wisdom has been that "they hate us because of our democracy, freedoms, culture, values, and success/advancement."

Yet, as we have discussed, the exact opposite is the case. Here is but a sampling of what some respondents have told us they admire most about the West:

> "I admire their freedom. They care for human rights. There is democracy and equality. They are well-developed in technology."
>
> — a Turkish respondent

"Real freedom, economic and scientific advancements, equality, justice."

— an Iranian

"The way they work hard. It has helped them in developing the country."

— a Pakistani

"Liberties and freedom and being open-minded with each other."

— a Moroccan

The common belief that Muslims are not open to others' ideas may originate from the widely published idea that anti-Americanism equals hatred of Western values and culture. However, Muslim responses to numerous open-ended questions lead in a different direction. In contrast to the 32% of Americans who say that they see nothing to admire about Muslims, the percentage of Muslims who say that they admire nothing about the West is significantly lower (6.3% in Jordan, 10% in Saudi Arabia, and 1% in Egypt).

As we have seen in the data, resentment against the West comes from what Muslims perceive as the West's hatred and denigration of Islam; the Western belief that Arabs and Muslims are inferior; and their fear of Western intervention, domination, or occupation. Given the power of the West and Western-dominated globalization (political, economic, and cultural), many may fear being overwhelmed by Western culture and losing their Muslim identity, independence, and values. Resentment among Muslims in the Middle East and North Africa in particular may come from the fact that while they admire the West's scientific and technological advancement as well as

> *Believing that the West would have to change its culture and values to improve relations with the Muslim world moves us in the wrong direction.*

its democracy, few believe the West is willing to allow them to have these same advantages. As one respondent from Saudi Arabia suggests: "Change the fact that countries in the Western world try to dominate the Islamic world rather than improve it."

So, believing that the West would have to change its culture and values to improve relations with the Muslim world moves us in the wrong direction.

Myth: We're Seeing the Clash of Civilizations

Looking at certain world events through Muslim eyes helps us understand the global anger and outrage that fueled the now-infamous cartoon controversy. Newspaper cartoons, including one depicting the Prophet Muhammad with a bomb in his turban — first published in Denmark in 2005 and then in other European cities — set off an international row in 2006. Protests erupted in an arc stretching from Europe through Africa to East Asia. Muslim journalists were arrested, and newspapers were closed for publishing the cartoons in Jordan, Algeria, and Yemen. European countries evacuated staffs of embassies and non-governmental organizations, and Muslim countries withdrew ambassadors.

The fallout also had economic repercussions. According to the *Gulf News*, Danish exports that had averaged more than $2.6 billion a year dried up as consumers in Muslim countries shunned Danish products in protest.[134] Danish dairy firm Arla Foods reported losing $1.5 million per day as a result of the regional consumer boycott that brought its sales to a standstill.

The cartoon controversy once again highlighted these questions: Is Islam incompatible with Western values? Are we seeing a clash of civilizations, a culture war? While many answer yes, others counter that the issue had little to do with a defense of Western democratic values and everything to do with a European media that reflects and plays to an increasingly xenophobic and Islamophobic society. Still others charge that the rush to reprint the Danish cartoons was as much about profits as about prophets.

Here again, data from the Gallup World Poll serve as a reality check on the causes for widespread outrage. As we have seen, a major complaint across Muslim societies is that the West denigrates Islam and Muslims and equates Islam with terrorism. The cartoons did not satirize or ridicule terrorists like Osama bin Laden or Abu Musab al-Zarqawi, but chose instead to satirize the venerated Prophet Muhammad, whom Muslims regard as the ideal model of Muslim life and values, in what was seen as a direct attack on Islam and a denigration of the faith.

Did Muslims react so strongly because they did not understand or believe in freedom of speech? Gallup's data, which demonstrate Muslim admiration for Western liberty and freedom of speech, indicate otherwise. The core issues of this apparent clash, or "culture war," are not democracy and freedom of expression, but faith, identity, respect (or lack of it), and public humiliation. As France's Grand Rabbi Joseph Sitruk observed in The Associated Press in the midst of the cartoon controversy: "We gain nothing by lowering religions, humiliating them and making caricatures of them. It's a lack of honesty and respect."

He further noted that freedom of expression "is not a right without limits."[135]

Many British and French citizens agree. Gallup's national representative polling in both countries shows that a majority of Britons (57%) and a plurality of the French (45%) say that newspapers printing a picture of the Prophet Muhammad should not be allowed under protection of free speech, while 35% and 40%, respectively, say it should be allowed. Britons and the French are even stronger in their disapproval of other expressions potentially covered by free speech: More than 75% of both populations say that a cartoon making light of the Holocaust should not be allowed under protection of free speech, and roughly 86% of the British and French public say the same about newspapers printing racial slurs. Clearly, for many European citizens, free speech is nuanced and contextual, not a black and white absolute.

Still, the issue of the cartoons was framed as a conflict between the absolute right of free speech in the liberal West and the violent intolerance of the Muslim world. This framing allowed non-representative groups on both sides to monopolize the debate and alienated moderate voices on both sides who call for closer relations and greater understanding between Muslim and Western communities. Inadvertently, the issue played directly into the hands of religious extremists and some autocratic rulers who charge that "Western" democracy is anti-religious and incompatible with Islam, while giving xenophobic and Islamophobic pundits yet more fuel to make the same claim.

Some observers have drawn a comparison between the Danish cartoon controversy and an incident from America's own cultural relations conflict: the 1965 Watts riots.

Often, U.S. policy makers and intellectuals draw an analogy between the Cold War and the current "global war on terror" and recommend analogous strategies because, after all, both conflicts battled over people's minds and hearts. But our analysis would point to important differences between the two conflicts and a danger in confusing them: In basic terms, the Cold War was about convincing people that communism was bad and that American democracy was good. The current war is about *not* appearing to denigrate Islam or impose a secular democracy that excludes Islam, because it is this very perception that fuels extremist sentiment and alienates those mainstream Muslims who want a democracy compatible with Islamic values.

The Cold War involved bringing down repressive communist governments in places such as Eastern Europe, where the ruling elites were largely unpopular with the people. The current war involves, at times, propping up unpopular repressive governments as a safeguard against the terrorists. Ironically, this very support fuels more animosity against the United States and thus empowers the violent extremists. Most importantly, many have claimed that "blue jeans and *Playboy*" brought down the Soviet Union as much as strong military deterrence. In sharp contrast, it is precisely America's military power and popular culture, and their perceived threat to Muslims, that extremists exploit to gain support. In short, much of what worked in the Cold War will have the opposite effect now.

Instead, another analogy, America's mistakes and triumphs in its own internal "clash of cultures" — the civil rights struggle — seems more appropriate. Some observers have drawn a comparison between the Danish cartoon controversy and an incident from America's own cultural relations conflict: the 1965 Watts riots. Looking at the cartoon controversy through the analogous lens of race relations reveals some insights. In both cases, violent riots broke out in reaction to what seemed to outsiders as a "petty offense." In the case of the Watts riots, white police officers in a predominantly black neighborhood pulled over two black males whom they believed were driving while intoxicated. In the case of the cartoons, a Danish newspaper, followed by other European newspapers, printed a cartoon depicting Islam's most venerated figure, the Prophet Muhammad, as a terrorist.

As a result of the Watts riots, 34 people were officially reported killed, more than 1,000 people were injured, and 4,000 people were arrested.[136] Six hundred buildings were damaged or destroyed, and an estimated $35 million in damage was caused (more than $150 million in today's currency).[137] Most of the physical damage was confined to businesses that had engendered resentment in the neighborhood because of their perceived unfair treatment of black people.

The Kerner Commission, set up by President Lyndon B. Johnson in 1967 to study the series of race riots, pointed to the distinction between the "trigger" (a petty act) and the "cause" — a long list of problems identified by the commission. These included poverty, job and housing discrimination, and unequal education, as well as a deep sense of racism and disrespect on the part of a powerful and affluent white America toward a powerless and poor black America — personified by the white police officers' treatment of the black men.

Several developments followed the commission's report and the violence that initiated it: Greater attention was paid to the grievances that the commission identified, which were not rendered void simply because people chose a violent way to protest them. Significantly, change occurred in two major areas. The first was policy: Laws were passed, and some were changed, to address these issues, such as the Civil Rights Act of 1968 prohibiting discrimination concerning the sale, rental, and financing of housing. The second was a greater cultural sensitivity: It slowly became less socially acceptable to use racist images of blacks in the media. For example, in 1966, CBS withdrew reruns of the *Amos 'n' Andy* show, which the National Association for the Advancement of Colored People (NAACP) had been protesting since the 1950s. Equally important, the media chose more frequently to quote constructive voices like Rev. Martin Luther King Jr., rather than emphasize extremist statements by Bobby Seale, co-founder of the Black Panthers, and others.

Was the NAACP protesting racist depictions of blacks because they didn't value free speech? Were rioters angry because they didn't understand the value of traffic laws? And were the corresponding changes on the part of U.S. media and government "concessions" to violence and intimidation by special interest groups or signs of a weakened American democracy and free speech? Some might argue yes, but others would see this as a natural progression of an increasingly inclusive American democracy, and that it is a better place today because of it.

Now, let's look at reactions in the United States to the Danish cartoon controversy. According to a 2006 Gallup Poll, most Americans (61%) said the controversy was due more to Muslims' intolerance of different points of view than to Western disrespect for Islam; interestingly, this percentage was even higher (73%) among those who reported watching the issue closely.[138] But, as discussed previously, many Muslims say they admire the West's principle of free speech. Moreover, large majorities in Muslim nations around the world say they would guarantee free speech — defined as allowing all citizens to express their opinion on the political, social, and economic issues of the day — if it was up to them to draft a constitution for a new country. However, like those who rioted in Watts and in other American cities during the country's civil rights struggle, Muslim rioters were not angry because they did not understand the value of free speech in principle. It was much more about who was enforcing this principle, in what way, and against whom — with what perceived motive.

For example, one Palestinian protester told an al-Jazeera reporter that European arguments about free speech were a double standard because in Germany, it was against the law to deny the Holocaust: "It's O.K. to offend Muslims but not Jews." Another blogger wrote that if freedom of individual expression was such a cherished value in Europe, why did it not extend to girls being allowed to wear whatever they wanted, including headscarves in French public schools?[139] Some have also pointed out that the same Danish editor who ran the original cartoon rejected a cartoon depicting Jesus Christ in an offensive manner because, as he explained to the cartoonists in an e-mail, there would be an "outcry" from his conservative readership.

> *It is clear that in the civil rights riots and the riots in the Muslim world, the protests were about much more than the "trigger" that set them off.*

Regardless of whether one agrees with or dismisses these arguments as "just different cases," it is clear that in the civil rights riots and the riots in the Muslim world, the protests were about much more than the "trigger" that set them off. Lessons learned from America's civil rights struggle help clarify how to begin to bridge the divide between the United States and the Muslim world. It will require change in two major areas: cultural sensitivity and listening to and understanding other people's points of view.

Cultural Sensitivity

Pope Benedict XVI and Islam

A September 12, 2006, address by Pope Benedict XVI at a university in Regensburg, Germany, triggered its own international reaction and protest across the Muslim world. This is astonishing because only four paragraphs of his eight-page text referred to Islam.[140] Particularly offensive to many Muslims was Benedict's citation of a 14th-century Byzantine emperor's remarks about the Prophet Muhammad: "Show me just what Muhammad brought that was new, and there you will find things only evil and inhuman, such as his command to spread by the sword the faith he preached."

Equally problematic and inaccurate was the pope's statement that the Quranic passage *"There is no compulsion in religion"* (Quran 2:256) was revealed in the early years of Muhammad's prophethood in Mecca, a period "when Mohammed was still powerless and under [threat]." But this concept, Benedict stated, was superseded or set aside later when Muhammad ruled

Medina by "instructions, developed later and recorded in the Quran, concerning holy war." To have the most promi-

One hundred leading Muslim scholars and leaders from around the world wrote and signed an open letter to the pope that explained the factual errors in his speech.

nent and influential Christian leader also apparently denigrate Islam and the Prophet and, although expressing regret that Muslims were offended, stop short of an apology, exacerbated the situation catalyzed by the Danish cartoons.

Morocco withdrew its ambassador to the Vatican; heads of state from Turkey to Indonesia voiced criticism; Egypt's senior religious leader, the Sheikh of al-Azhar, commented on the pope's ignorance of Islam; and leaders of Muslim organizations called for a public apology.

One hundred leading Muslim scholars and leaders from around the world wrote and signed an open letter to the pope that explained the factual errors in his speech:[141]

> You mention that "according to the experts" the verse which begins, *There is no compulsion in religion* (al-Baqarah 2:256) is from the early period when the Prophet "was still powerless and under threat," but this is incorrect. In fact this verse is acknowledged to belong to the period of Qur'anic revelation corresponding to the political and military ascendance of the young Muslim community.

> We would like to point out that "holy war" is a term that does not exist in Islamic languages. *Jihad*, it must be emphasized, means struggle, and specifically struggle in the way of God. This struggle may take many forms, including the use of

force. Though a *jihad* may be *sacred* in the sense of being directed towards a sacred ideal, it is not necessarily a "war."

You say that "naturally the emperor knew the instructions, developed later and recorded in the Qur'an, concerning holy war." However, as we pointed out above concerning *There is no compulsion in religion*, the aforementioned instructions were not later at all. Moreover, the emperor's statements about violent conversion show that he did not know what those instructions are and have always been.

The pope's speech resulted in public demonstrations, the burning of the pope in effigy in Pakistan, and sporadic acts of violence against Christians and Christian churches. Violent extremists aside, why was there such widespread concern among so many mainstream Muslims?

Muslim responses need to be understood within the context of a world in which many Muslims feel under siege. Commenting on the cartoon controversy and the pope's remarks in *Javan*, an Iranian newspaper, Mohammad Reza Jamali writes:

If we look at the situation carefully, we would see that not only is the era of colonialism and all that it entails not over, but amazingly enough it has come to plunder the material and spiritual resources of the oppressed peoples of the world in a new disguise. The greatest obstacle to colonialism today is the wave of Islamic awakening that has risen from Islamic teachings. It is for this reason that in their new division of labour colonialists are targeting Islam and are insulting sacred Islamic beliefs.

> *At the heart of the problem is the tendency to believe that a monolithic West is pitted against a monolithic Muslim world.*

The recent offensive statements by the pope and the offensive cartoons that were published a few months ago all serve this very purpose. If Muslims and freedom-loving people everywhere fail to voice their fervent protests and do not condemn these actions, then we predict a rise in this kind of undertakings in the future.

Understanding Muslim public opinion can be a key to pre-empting or preventing conflict in today's world, making it easier to anticipate and to avoid unnecessary conflicts. If we place Benedict's speech at Regensburg — as well as the Danish cartoons — within the context of Muslim responses in the Gallup World Poll data, Muslim reactions are predictable and the conflicts avoidable.

The West vs. the Muslim World?

At the heart of the problem is the tendency to believe that a monolithic West — a coherent unit defined by democracy, human rights, gender equality, and the division of church and state (secularism) — is pitted against a monolithic Muslim world that has sharply different values and aspirations that are incompatible with "Western" values.

Western countries exhibit great diversity. The robust presence and role of religion in the United States differs significantly from the decline of religion in Europe in countries such as Britain, France, and Germany or the Scandinavian countries. U.S. separation of church and state contrasts with Britain, Germany, and Norway, which still have state religions and/or state support for religious institutions. Ironically, American publics are much more religious than European publics (68% of Americans vs. 28% of Britons, for example, say that religion is an important part of their lives). At the same time, in the United States, where church and state are separated by law, a majority says it favors the Bible as "a source" of legislation (55%) — of that, 9% say it should be "the only source."

Other significant differences are evident in the broad disagreement among European nations about going to war in Iraq. U.S. and British military engagement sharply contrasts with major allies such as France and Germany, who were not supportive, and Spain and Italy, who were initially supportive but then bent to pressure from their majorities and pulled out of Iraq. Finally, Western European nations share most of the Muslim world's negative opinion of U.S. leadership: 68% of Germans, 67% of French, and even 52% of Britons disapprove of U.S. leadership, as do 62% of Jordanians and 53% of Turks.

There is also wide diversity among Muslim nations — politically, economically, culturally, and religiously. As discussed earlier, oil-rich and rapidly developing Gulf states such as Qatar, the United Arab Emirates, and Saudi Arabia hardly resemble poor, struggling, underdeveloped countries such as Mali and Yemen. Islamic republics such as Iran contrast sharply with the more secular-oriented governments of Egypt and Syria. Arab and Muslim nations have a history of rivalry and conflict: Saddam's Iraq versus Iran, Iraq versus the Gulf states, and Egypt versus Sudan. We also forget the vast cultural differences among Muslims: Less than a quarter are Arab; the majority of Muslims are Asian or African. Finally, significant religious differences exist between Sunni and Shia Muslims who, despite their common Islamic faith, have critical theological and political differences and religious orientations that range from ultra-orthodox to liberal reformers.

The surprising conclusion? Muslims globally, like people of many other faiths, are geographically, racially, linguistically, and culturally diverse.

To the further surprise of many, even in terms of some values, Muslims show substantial diversity. For example, only 27% of Jordanians and 33% of Saudis say divorce "cannot be morally justified," while 46% of Egyptians and 92% of Bangladeshis assign divorce this label. This difference among Muslims not only illustrates how diverse Muslims are as people with varying cultures and norms, but it also exemplifies the rich diversity within Islam's schools of thought, which hold differing opinions on the issue of divorce.

Muslims and the West: Shared Concerns

In contrast to expected differences, the number of commonalities we find between the Muslim world and the West shatters many myths. A significant number of Americans and Muslims believe that religion is or ought to be a pillar of their society, informed and guided by the Bible or *Sharia*. Majorities of both groups cite the importance of religion in public life and the preservation of family values. Each group is concerned about its economic future, employment and jobs, and the ability to support its families. Each gives high priority to technology,

The more Americans report knowing about Muslim countries, the more likely they are to hold positive views of those countries.

democracy, the importance of broad political participation, and freedoms of speech and social justice. Both strongly support eradicating extremism.

Do Americans Understand Muslims?

Unfortunately, Americans' feelings or beliefs about Muslims reflect little of the above data:

- Forty-four percent of Americans say Muslims are too extreme in their religious beliefs. Less than half believe that U.S. Muslims are loyal to the United States.

- Nearly one-quarter of Americans, 22%, say they would not want a Muslim as a neighbor. As we have seen, 32% of Americans say they admire nothing about the Muslim world, and 25% admit they simply "don't know."

What's even more surprising is that Americans' self-reported knowledge of Muslim views did not change from 2002 to 2007 despite (or perhaps because of) the dramatic spike in media coverage of the Muslim world during this time.[142] A majority (57%) say they know either nothing or not much about "the opinions and beliefs of people who live in Muslim countries." Interestingly, the more Americans report knowing about Muslim countries, the more likely they are to hold positive views of those countries. This same trend is found as it relates to knowing a Muslim: Those Americans who know at least one Muslim are more likely to hold positive views of Muslims and Islam.[143]

Americans say what they admire least about the Muslim world is extremism, radicalism, lack of openness to others' ideas, and gender inequality.

Muslims show substantial agreement with two of the above concerns — condemning the "radical fringe" and citing lack of openness to others' ideas as what they admire least about their own societies. However, Muslim and American perceptions diverge sharply on the issue of gender inequality among Muslims. For Muslim women, half of the population polled, this concern is almost absent in criticism of their societies. Blaming Islam for women's mistreatment is a losing strategy that alienates those who would otherwise support an end to violence and women's oppression and empowers those who oppose women's rights in the name of defending Islam against a West who hates and wants to destroy the faith.

Then, Why Do They Hate Us?

As our data have demonstrated, the primary cause of broad-based anger and anti-Americanism is not a clash of civilizations but the perceived effect of U.S. foreign policy in the Muslim world. Nor is there a blind hatred of the West.

- Muslim opinion distinguishes between Western nations and between their leaders: America/Bush and Britain/Blair vs. France/Chirac and Germany (Blair and Chirac were still in office when Gallup conducted this poll).

- Unfavorable opinions of Britain and the United States contrast sharply with more positive opinions of France and Germany. Across all predominantly Muslim countries polled, an average of 75% of respondents associate "ruthless" with the United States (in contrast to only 13% for France and 13% for Germany).

- Western European nations share Muslim opinions about the United States.

Thus, we need to disaggregate "the West" and the "Muslim world" into individual, distinct countries whose confrontations and conflicts are attributable to specific policies of specific nations and their leaders, especially the United States. While knowing more about Muslims makes Americans more likely to hold positive views about them, the exact opposite trend exists among Muslims with regard to their opinion of the U.S. government. The closer that respondents follow news about issues related to U.S. foreign policy, the more likely they are to hold negative opinions of the U.S. government.[144]

Mutual Misperceptions: "They Just Don't Care"

Further reinforcing the attitudinal divide between the West and Muslim nations is the mutual perception, or more correctly misperception, that significant percentages on both sides believe the other side does not care. However, data show that only minorities on both sides are unconcerned about better relations between the West and Muslim societies, revealing a clash of ignorance rather than a clash of civilizations.

A top American response to what they least admire about Muslims is that Muslims are not motivated to be a part of, or have relations with, the rest of the world. However, in sharp contrast, one of the statements Muslim respondents most frequently associate with their own societies is "eager to have better relations with the West."

> *Although many Muslims believe that the West does not show concern for better relations with them, only 11% of Americans say that better relations between the West and the Islamic world do not concern them, contradicting the popular Muslim notion of "apathetic Americans."*

In most countries surveyed, the percentage who say that a better understanding between Western and Muslim cultures concerns them a lot significantly outnumbers the percentage who say it does not concern them. In some cases, as with Saudi Arabia, Morocco, and Lebanon, those who are concerned outnumber those who are not by a ratio of 2 to 1. Similarly, although many Muslims believe that the West does not show concern for better relations with them, only 11% of Americans say that better relations between the West and the Islamic world do not concern them, contradicting the popular Muslim notion of "apathetic Americans."

What Should Be Done?

A majority of Americans say that relations with the Muslim world concern them a lot and believe that more interaction is necessary. At the same time, they also indicate that they don't know what to admire about the Muslim world. Demonstrating mutual frustration, a top response from both the Muslim world and Americans regarding what can be done to improve relations is "I don't know" or "nothing."

Americans who have recommendations on ways to improve relations emphasize the need to correct Muslim perceptions or
misperceptions of the West (improve education and communi-
cation) or to correct Muslim behavior (control or stop extremists). Americans' solutions for improving relations stop here.
They do not mention the need to address or review U.S. foreign
policy, but seem to think that whatever rift exists between the
West and Muslim nations is one of mutual cultural misunderstanding as well as Muslim extremism. In a January 2007
Gallup Poll, 8 in 10 Americans say they believe that people in
Muslim countries have an unfavorable opinion of them, and
the majority (57%) say it is because of "misinformation" about
American actions, while only 26% say it is because of what the
United States has actually done. This percentage is down from
March 2002, when almost 8 in 10 said that misinformation was
the root of Muslim antipathy.

Muslims also characterize whatever rift exists between the
West and Muslim nations as one of lack of understanding and
mutual respect, but they add the need for a change in behavior
and policy on *both* sides. However, contrary to what the "They
Hate Our Freedom" thesis might predict, Muslims do not recommend or insist upon changes to Western culture or social
norms as the path to better relations. While the breakdown
of social morals is an aspect they resent most about the West,
rectifying this is not cited as a way to improve relations. Rather,
they call on the West to show greater respect for Islam, and
they emphasize policy-related issues:

- adopt practical policies to help the economic development of Muslim nations

- refrain from interfering in the internal affairs of Muslim states and from imposing beliefs and policies

- and, especially among the Arab states, adopt a fair stance toward Palestine

In contrast to Americans, Muslims do recommend changes in actions on *their* part to improve relations with the West. Responses include: "respect the West's positive thinking and values like freedom of speech and religion"; "reduce/control extremism and terrorism"; and "modernize and be open to the West's positive thinking; take the good, leave the bad." Respondents perceive that Western policy toward Muslims is being fueled, at least in part, by the West's disrespect for Islam as well as exploitive economic or political agendas. Thus, they believe it is important for Muslims to "improve the presentation of Islam" as a possible solution to improve relations with the West — also perhaps to do their part in promoting the "respect for Islam" they are demanding from the West.

The United States' role in Muslim-West relations, on the other hand, shows a potentially dangerous complacency, given America's status as the world's sole superpower. Thirty-eight percent — a relatively large number of Americans — say they don't know what the West could do to improve Muslim-West relations or believe that there is nothing else that can be done to improve relations. At the same time, contrary to the common charge, significant numbers of Muslims do not simply blame the West. Muslim respondents believe it is primarily the responsibility of the Muslim world to stop extremism and terrorism.

> *Islam may be a powerful weapon for discrediting terrorists and limiting the growth of terrorism.*

Targeting Islam as the Problem?

Some in the West counsel that Islam is the problem and that the West needs to fight it or create a "moderate Islam" to defeat anti-Americanism, overcome resistance to modernization, and promote democracy and human rights. This rhetoric alienates the very Muslim majorities that are Western allies in the fight against religious extremism and global terrorism. This approach can result in unwise foreign policies: support for secular authoritarian leaders and regimes that suppress all opposition, including mainstream secular leaders and "Muslim democrats"; the marginalization of mainstream Islamic parties that function within society; and a "shock and awe" military policy to promote democracy. It also results in domestic policies that compromise civil liberties: indiscriminate profiling and arrest of Muslims, monitoring of mosques, and closure of religious institutions. The net result is to convince many Muslims that the West is waging a war against Islam and Muslims.

The problem is not Islam any more than Christianity or Judaism is the cause of its extremists and terrorists; it's the political radicalization of religion that creates militant theologies. Islam may be a powerful weapon for discrediting terrorists and limiting the growth of terrorism. For example, in Indonesia, those who say that 9/11 was unjustified support this response by citing religious principles ("It is against God's law," "God hates murder," or "It is against Islam") as well as humanitarian ones (the loss of human life was tragic, and so forth), while those who say that 9/11 was justified cite *political grievances* to support their response, not religious justifications.

For overwhelming majorities of Muslims (who are also the moderates), Islam is a fundamental source of identity, guidance, and spiritual and psychological security. Mainstream Muslims, who have been the primary victims of terrorism, are as concerned about extremism, violence, and terror as are Westerners. They, even more than Westerners, believe that they are responsible for fighting extremism and for modernizing their societies. Respecting Islam will encourage the moderate majority to use their authentic interpretation and engagement of religion to disarm the extremists by using the Quran's principles against terrorism.

Regarding religion as the primary problem weakens the positive power of religion and culture and obscures our common values and shared concerns. This fear of Islam leads to the belief in a monolithic Islamic threat that requires massive Western political and military power. Our over-reliance on military solutions is then seen by many Muslims not as an effort to liberate and democratize, but to occupy and dominate — in essence, to "redraw the map of the Middle East and Muslim world."

The perception of U.S. policy as a form of American neo-colonialism — what a prominent group of neoconservatives has called the creation of a New American Century — fuels anti-Americanism globally in the Muslim world and beyond and is used by terrorists as they appeal to new recruits. It also diminishes American moral authority in the Muslim world, Europe, and other parts of the world. Lastly, it silences the voices of moderate Muslims who advocate better relations with the United States.

So what should be done?

> *Government leaders and politicians use and abuse religion in domestic and international politics, too often talking about and for Muslims who have not been heard.*

Public Diplomacy: Winning Minds and Hearts

The Gallup World Poll consistently confirms that the crucial issues in improving relations are the beliefs and perceptions of "the other," which affect and need to inform foreign policies. The war against global terrorism has been fought on three major fronts: military, economic, and diplomatic. As military experts have noted, while the military can capture and kill terrorists, it is not equipped to win the struggle for minds and hearts. This, many today would argue, requires a public diplomacy that addresses the ideological dimensions of war: the war of ideas and the foreign policies created.

Government agencies, think tanks, and the military — all of which in the past had ignored the relationship of religion to politics and international affairs — now have special units of experts, conferences, workshops, and curricula focusing on Islam and Muslim politics and culture. Government leaders and politicians use and abuse religion in domestic and international politics, too often talking about and for Muslims who have not been heard. Few are able to base their conclusions on data-driven analysis that reflects the voices of majorities of Muslims across the world — data that are vital in a campaign of programs and policies to win hearts and minds.

Conclusion

While Gallup data indicate that faith is not the distinguishing factor primarily responsible for extremism, Islam does remain

a significant source of religious, historical, national, and cultural identity. Thus, Islam remains in the spotlight. As noted in Chapter 2, secular and religious rulers and reform and opposition movements (mainstream and extremist) have used religion to legitimate, recruit, mobilize, and motivate. Just as religion remains part of the fabric of Muslim societies, so too it remains a potent force in political and social change.

As we have seen, both our data and Muslim politics demonstrate a broad-based desire for greater political participation, democratization, government accountability, and the rule of law. However, a major concern in the region is that the West is not really interested in Muslim self-determination, but instead desires to bolster authoritarian regimes and promote its own brand of democratic governance. In the short run, real self-determination will require engaging religious political parties and leaders who would be democratically elected if free and fair elections were held in many countries today. Many will be more independent and disagree with some U.S. policies. However, allowing people to make change peacefully and air their grievances freely will diminish the allure of those who advocate violence as the only means available. Moreover, opening up the political system in countries where strong political parties have not been permitted will also provide non-Islamist alternatives.

Diagnosing terrorism as a symptom and Islam as the problem, though popular in some circles, is flawed and has serious risks with dangerous repercussions. It confirms radical beliefs and fears, alienates the moderate Muslim majority, and reinforces a belief that the war against global terrorism is really a war against Islam. Whether one is radical or moderate, this negative attitude is a widespread perception.

Muslims say that they admire Western technology and liberty most of all, and then go on to say that they associate these qualities most not with France, Japan, or Germany, but with the United States. It is precisely because the West in general, and the United States in particular, is seen as having "a fair judicial system," as giving its "own citizens many liberties," and portraying itself as a champion of human rights that U.S. actions toward Muslims, such as those at Guantanamo, Abu Ghraib, and other abuses are seen as so hypocritical.

One U.S. diplomat who was in Egypt when the Abu Ghraib scandal broke out said she was told by the locals: "We would expect this from our own government, but not from you." Ironically, it may be because of America's idealized image as a beacon for democracy in the Muslim world that its actions elicit such passionate anger. The perception is: For you, America, to go against your own values and how you would treat your own people and to abuse Muslims in this way means you must *really* despise us and our faith.

Avoiding or ending acute conflicts in the Muslim world is more effective than projecting a strong military presence to safeguard American interests and limit the growth of global terrorism. The argument that a strong military presence in the region will win the war against terrorism is not borne out by Gallup data from across the Muslim world. The long war against terror will not be won on the battlefield, but by winning the loyalty of the people in the region. While terrorists must be fought aggressively, military occupation of Muslim lands increases anti-American sentiment, diminishes American moral authority with allies, and silences the voices of moderates who want better relations.

In the end, ongoing conflict between the West and the Muslim world is not inevitable. It is about policy, not a clash of principles. Polls found that Lebanese hold Christians and Muslims in high regard (more than 90% have favorable opinions of each)[145] despite a decades-long civil war in Lebanon fought roughly along confessional lines. Today, less than a generation after the civil rights struggle, a majority of blacks and whites in America say that relations between their groups are good.[146] These hopeful examples underscore the possibility of improving relations between groups — even those whose conflicts lasted centuries — and the relative speed by which this is possible when there is a greater understanding of the conflict's root cause.

Acknowledgements

On behalf of John and myself, I would like to thank the following people for contributing to *Who Speaks for Islam?* Our book
presents the efforts and knowledge of hundreds of great minds.

First, I'd like to thank Dr. Jean Esposito for her tremendous
help in the creation of this book. Her insight, strategic thinking,
analysis, and patience were the bedrock of our team effort. She
is truly a co-creator and co-author, as well as a dear friend and
partner.

I would also like to thank my husband and best friend, Dr.
Mohamed Foraida, whose support, sacrifice, patience, and passion made this book possible. I would also extend this gratitude
to my two boys, Tariq and Jibreel, who keep me laughing and
dreaming.

From both a personal and professional perspective, I want to
recognize the many in the Gallup tribe who helped build the
massive research base described in this book, starting with our
Chairman and CEO, Jim Clifton, whose vision and leadership
made the World Poll a reality. Dr. Gale Muller, our chief sci-
entist, turned a dream of hearing the voices of 6 billion world
citizens into hundreds of thousands of megabits of data. Richard
Burkholder, director of international polling; Alec Gallup; and
Jihad Fakhreddine together began this important work in 2001
when everyone told us it was impossible.

Hearing the voices of a billion Muslims could not have been possible without the massive effort of our research team. It was truly a privilege to work with this group, who are some of the greatest scientists and methodologists in the world. These researchers went into far reaches of the Earth — into the most remote rural villages in Asia, Africa, and the former Soviet Union to give every person a voice, not just those conveniently located in an urban center. Thank you to Dr. Rajesh Srinivasan, Dr. Bob Tortora, and Neli Esipova for their brilliance and hard work. I would also like to recognize Dr. Zsolt Nyiri for his groundbreaking work surveying Muslims in Europe and to Dr. Frank Newport for his ongoing excellence in polling the American public.

Our analytical team was key in the development of this book: Eric Olesen, Raksha Arora, Matt Webber, Lydia Saad, Hadia Mubarak, Dr. Jeff Jones, Dr. Glenn Phelps, and the many others who lent their analysis and insight to the discoveries this book presents. Our team of material researchers: Hadia again, Nura Jandali, Yasmin Mogahed, Mona Mogahed, and Paul Scott, who contributed to the context that makes the numbers relevant, were vital in the development of this work.

The team of editors, designers, and publishing executives was critical. Larry Emond conceptualized a book that would tell the world what a billion Muslims really think. Dr. Piotr Juszkiewicz has done a marvelous job of getting this book out to the world. Beth Karadeema created a superb and very readable design. And Julie Ray, Geoff Brewer, and Kelly Henry provided rigorous editing and insightful suggestions.

APPENDIX A: METHODOLOGICAL DESIGN AND SAMPLING

Methodological Design

The Gallup World Poll uses two primary methodological designs:

- A Random-Digit-Dial (RDD) telephone survey design is used in countries where 80% or more of the population has landline phones. This situation is typical in the United States, Canada, Western Europe, Japan, Australia, etc.

- In the developing world, including much of Latin America, the former Soviet Union countries, nearly all of Asia, the Middle East, and Africa, an area frame design is used for face-to-face interviewing.

The following are key aspects of the overall Gallup World Poll survey philosophy:

- The sample represents all parts of each country*, including all rural areas.

- Countries are reviewed on a case-by-case basis when part of a country cannot be included in the sample design. The review determines whether the survey should be carried out.

---

*Three exceptions exist: Areas that threaten the safety of interviewing staff are excluded, as are scarcely populated islands in some countries and areas that can be reached only by foot or by animal, with the exception of China.

- The target population includes all individuals aged 15 and older.

- Face-to-face interviews are approximately one hour in length. Telephone interviews are considerably shorter, about 30 minutes in length.

- There is a standard set of questions used around the world.

- In the parts of the world where face-to-face surveys are conducted, the questionnaire includes questions tailored to each region. For example, the questions used in heavily indebted poor countries are tailored toward providing information about progress on the Millennium Development Goals.

- The questionnaire is translated* into the major languages of each country.

- Interviewing supervisors and interviewers are trained not only on the questionnaire, but also on the execution of field procedures. This interviewing training usually takes place in a central location.

- Quality control procedures are used to validate that correct samples are selected and that the correct person is randomly selected in each household. Random respondent selection uses either the latest birthday method or the Kish Grid.

---

*The translation process includes two independent translations and back translations; survey personnel adjudicate the differences.

Sampling

The typical World Poll survey in a country consists of 1,000 completed questionnaires. However, in some countries, over-samples may be collected in major cities. For example, we collected an additional 500 interviews in Moscow.

In countries where face-to-face surveys are conducted, census listings of Primary Sampling Units (PSU), consisting of clusters of households, are the main way of selecting the sample. Typically, the PSU are stratified this way:

I.   Cities with population = 1,000,000 or more

II. Cities with population = 500,000 to 999,999

III. Cities with population = 100,000 to 499,999

IV. Cities with population = 50,000 to 99,999

V.   Towns with population = 10,000 to 49,999

VI. Towns/Rural villages with populations under 10,000

PSU are proportionally allocated to the population in each stratum, and typically 125 PSU are sampled with an average of eight interviews, one interview per sampled household, per PSU. If maps of the PSU are available, then they are used; otherwise, the selected PSU must be mapped. Random route procedures are used to select sampled households. Interviewers must make at least three attempts to survey the sampled household, unless an outright refusal occurs. If an interview cannot be obtained at the initial sampled household, the household to the immediate right of the initial household is selected. If the first attempt at this household is unsuccessful, then the house immediately to the left of the initial household is selected. Attempts to obtain an interview can be made at up to nine households.

In the RDD survey, at least five call attempts are made to reach a person, aged 15 and older, in each household. Typically the design is not stratified, but otherwise, the other processes and procedures follow those used in the face-to-face design.

Statistical Validity

The first round of data collection was carried out in late 2005 and 2006. These probability surveys are valid* within a statistical margin of error, also called a 95% confidence interval. This means that if the survey is conducted 100 times using the exact same procedures, the margin of error would include the "true value" in 95 out of the 100 surveys. With a sample size of 1,000, the margin of error for a percentage at 50% is ±3 percentage points.

Because these surveys use a clustered sample design, the margin of error varies by question, and if a user is making critical decisions based on the margin of error, he or she should consider inflating the margin of error by the design effect. The design effect accounts for the potential of correlated responses, and increase in the margin of error, caused by the sample of clusters of households in PSU.

---

*Assuming other sources of error, such as non-response, by some members of the targeted sample are equal. Other errors that can affect survey validity include measurement error associated with the questionnaire, such as translation issues and coverage error, where a part or parts of the target population aged 15 and older have a zero probability of being selected for the survey.

World Poll Country List

Afghanistan	Canada	Guatemala
Albania	Chad	Haiti
Algeria	Chile	Honduras
Angola	China	Hungary
Argentina	Colombia	India
Armenia	Costa Rica	Indonesia
Australia	Croatia	Iran
Austria	Cuba	Iraq
Azerbaijan	Cyprus	Ireland
Bangladesh	Czech Republic	Israel
Belarus	Denmark	Italy
Belgium	Dominican Republic	Jamaica
Benin	Ecuador	Japan
Bolivia	Egypt	Jordan
Bosnia and Herzegovina	El Salvador	Kazakhstan
	Estonia	Kenya
Botswana	Ethiopia	Kosovo
Brazil	Finland	Kuwait
Bulgaria	France	Kyrgyzstan
Burkina Faso	Georgia	Latvia
Burundi	Germany	Lebanon
Cambodia	Ghana	Lithuania
Cameroon	Greece	Macedonia

Continued on next page

World Poll Country List (*continued*)

Madagascar	Peru	Taiwan, Province of China
Malawi	Philippines	Tajikistan
Malaysia	Poland	Tanzania
Mali	Portugal	Thailand
Mauritania	Puerto Rico	Togo
Mexico	Romania	Trinidad & Tobago
Moldova	Russia	Tunisia
Montenegro	Rwanda	Turkey
Morocco	Saudi Arabia	Uganda
Mozambique	Senegal	Ukraine
Myanmar (Burma)	Serbia	United Arab Emirates
Nepal	Sierra Leone	United Kingdom
Netherlands	Singapore	Uruguay
New Zealand	Slovakia	USA
Nicaragua	Slovenia	Uzbekistan
Niger	South Africa	Venezuela
Nigeria	South Korea	Vietnam
Norway	Spain	Yemen
Pakistan	Sri Lanka	Zambia
Palestinian Territory	Sudan	Zimbabwe
Panama	Sweden	
Paraguay	Switzerland	

Country list subject to change

APPENDIX B: **THE GALLUP JOURNEY TO POLL THE WORLD**

In the wake of 9/11, Gallup married its expertise in global social science research and its management consulting to create The Gallup Global Institute. Following Gallup's tradition of data-driven analysis, the institute's first task was to conduct the largest ever social science research endeavor, the Gallup World Poll. The World Poll is an ongoing survey of respondents in more than 130 countries and areas, and its results are representative of 95% of the world's population. The Gallup Poll of the Muslim World, the basis for the findings presented in this book, is part of this initiative.

The Gallup World Poll is a self-funded study conducted purely for research — not advocacy — purposes. Gallup has never done polling for any political party or advocacy group, and it never will. The purity and objectivity of the data and analysis are the foundation of Gallup's business model and the core of its brand.

Here are the highlights of the particular journey Gallup took to create this book.

Phase 1: Envisioning the "Impossible"
Richard Burkholder, Gallup's director of international polling — or as he's called around Gallup, our very own Indiana Jones — likes to refer to a Reuters article from October 2001:

"In tightly controlled countries where absolute rule by royal or princely families is the norm, systematic research such as published political opinion polls is still taboo," the article reads. "The inherent conservatism of these societies means the advent of such research, if it happens, will be slow."

Despite the skepticism of regional experts, Gallup decided the project was too important not to try.

Phase 2: Questionnaire Design — Picking Through the Thorns

"The mere formulation of a problem is far more often essential than its solution. To raise new questions, new possibilities, to regard old problems from a new angle, requires creative imagination and marks real advances in science."

— Albert Einstein

Gallup went into this research assuming nothing. Researchers deliberately avoided taking popularly held notions as "givens." This may seem like a subtle point, but survey questionnaire design is a delicate art. For questions to be as objective as possible, researchers must acknowledge their implicit assumptions about a given topic and write questions that carefully avoid inadvertently leading the respondent. For example, when Gallup studied European Muslims, it did not design the questionnaire assuming that "integration" was the panacea for radicalism. It instead asked questions measuring each dimension and let the data reveal whether the correlation between integration and moderation was real.

That said, writing the right questions would take more than a passion for scientific rigor. There were two important constituencies to consider in developing the questionnaire: the government authorities in each of the countries surveyed and the respondents themselves.

"The risks were always there in the sense of treading into politically sensitive territories," Jihad Fakhreddine notes. Fakhreddine, Gallup's partner in the region, co-created Gallup's first questionnaire. "As Arab researchers, we felt that we knew the limits, but with this research we wanted to test those limits. That latter goal was the most interesting and rewarding intellectually, and, I would say, from a business perspective as well."

In early November 2001, Burkholder and Fakhreddine sat down in Dubai day after day to carve out the questionnaire. They walked a fine line, striving to anticipate the concerns of government officials. By focusing on the respondents' worldview, making it clear that the primary goal of the study was to reach a better understanding of their values and beliefs, they were able to couch indirect questions about terrorism and the West in a straightforward, innocuous context.

The strategy worked — at least in most cases. In several countries, the final questionnaire cleared local officials with little trouble, while in others, officials indicated that it would be acceptable with minor adjustments. In Saudi Arabia, a country crucial to the study because of its status as the spiritual center of the Muslim world, officials were especially resistant, insisting that key questions be changed or dropped.

"Approval came very late there, and it only happened because Sami [Pan Arab Research Center (PARC) president] was so persistent," Burkholder says. "Finally, he called me, delighted, from the airport in Jiddah [Saudi Arabia] to tell me we'd pulled it off."

Phase 3: "They'll never want to talk to you"

Perhaps an even more difficult hurdle than obtaining government permission in each of the countries was earning the trust of the participants themselves. "The tricky part was constructing the questionnaire so respondents wouldn't be circumspect in expressing what they really felt," Burkholder says. "The risk-averse thing would be to say, 'Whatever the party line is, that goes for me too.'"

The researchers addressed that problem by starting with banal questions, such as the types of books and newspapers respondents like to read. The questionnaire then progressed gradually to general items about values important to respondents, then to general questions on their opinions of Western value systems, and finally to more specific questions about their opinions of the West. "We saved the tough stuff for late in the interview," Burkholder notes.

Burkholder recalls when he was in Baghdad in early July 2003 to conduct research on the views of Iraqis after the coalition invasion. He met with a newly appointed Iraqi official inside the Green Zone and was told: "These people are closed to outsiders. You'll never get them to talk to you." Understandably, Burkholder started to feel a bit discouraged, as he had flown all this way to be turned back by what presumably would be a very high non-response bias (survey-speak for when no one wants to be interviewed). After the official left, a New Zealander who had overheard the conversation said, "I wouldn't pay too much attention to what he said, mate. He's been in Minneapolis for the past 20 years." And he was right on both counts. That summer in Iraq, Burkholder managed to get a response rate of more than 95% (for reference, Gallup is having a good day when it gets a 50% response rate in the United States).

Asked how he does it, Burkholder starts to sound more like a psychologist than a survey researcher: "It's about building trust. No matter how well you craft the questions, create a perfect sampling plan, train the interviewers, if the respondent doesn't think you are sincere, you'll never get them to open up." The moment of truth, Burkholder explains, is when the respondents realize you really care about their views, as he witnessed first-hand during an interview in Lebanon:

"There was a young woman, maybe in her early 30s, in a tough neighborhood in Beirut. Her husband wanted to be overbearing — he kept interrupting and trying to coach her, but the interviewer politely ignored him, so the wife finally got it that it was *her* answers we were interested in. Her responses to the open-ended questions were extremely eloquent. We asked about the meaning of four or five aspects of life — like 'What does family mean to you?' She said something like, 'Well, it's life.' We asked, 'What does spiritual struggle mean to you?' 'It's the thing that makes life possible.' She thought a long time about each one, and she gave responses that were almost poetic. It was fascinating to listen to her."

Did Burkholder ever feel threatened? Kuwait registered some of the most anti-American sentiment of the nine countries studied in the first wave. Burkholder visited several respondents' homes there to sit in on interviews during the pre-testing phase (interviews at which Burkholder was present were not used in the analysis). "It's a little nerve-racking to go into some of these tough neighborhoods as a Westerner," he says. "They were very gracious once you were in their place, but it felt like I was kind of stretching it to be there."

However, residents seemed to make a clear distinction between resentment toward Western policies and disrespect toward individuals from the West. "I never felt hostility personally," Burkholder says of his trip to Kuwait. "Historically, people have noticed they're extremely hospitable people — it's hard to get out of their houses! And it was fascinating to watch them be interviewed. They were very passionate in their responses because they are highly politicized."

Burkholder also says that several residents shared connections they had with the West. "I would have these little surprises. I was in one really tough neighborhood in a worker area — the [respondent] happened to be a Kuwaiti national, but almost everyone else in the area wasn't. At one point, he said, 'Here's my son; he was born in Nashville.' I was like, 'What?' He said, 'Well, actually my other son had a problem with his spleen, and the government would pay for us to have it fixed. So we flew to the U.S. for the operation; my other son was born there.'"

But there were also constant reminders of distinctions between the Muslim and Western worlds. Burkholder remembers that feeling being particularly acute in Lebanon. "That was a fascinating trip because it's one of these places that's kind of on the fault line between Islam and the West," he says. "Forty-two percent or so of the population is Christian, and 57% is Muslim — they're within the same political entity, but 15 years ago, they were killing each other with a passion that would make Belfast look like a Grange meeting. You could see it physically on the buildings. But there's enough cross-pollination going on now that at least within the professional sector, there's some normality to it."

Iran was one of the few countries in which female interviewers could be used — a condition ironically made necessary by Iran's conservative culture. Female respondents could not speak to male interviewers. "They do need female interviewers to interview women," Burkholder notes, "but they have to be completely compartmentalized from their male colleagues. That was a big reminder that it's a very different environment."

Phase 4: Letting the Data Drive

Once Gallup had the data — mountains and mountains of it — the fun started for the researchers: digging into the numbers and uncovering the patterns beneath the apparent chaos. What mysteries could the data help Gallup solve? Researchers turned their attention to a deep analysis of the findings. First, they examined the time trends of nations they had surveyed in 2001 vs. 2005-2007. What had changed? What had endured? They looked at everything from views of the United States to level of personal piety. They made note of especially high and low levels in a particular country and tried to find out the reasons why by looking at other parts of the survey. They investigated apparent contradictions — where the data say that two things that seem like mutually exclusive opposites are true at the same time.

The researchers often discovered their most valuable pearls in their resolution of the contradictions. For example, women in many nations say they favor gender equality and associate this value with the West, but at the same time, do not favor adopting Western values. The resolution of this apparent conflict resulted in a valuable insight into gender justice as understood by many Muslims: While Muslim women believe in gender legal equality, they see the West's perceived moral laxness as socially degrading to women. The implication is that coupling women's liberation movements with Madonna alienates the very people these efforts seek to help.

In Gallup's research, what researchers *didn't* find became as important as what they did find. For example:

- Gallup found no significant difference between women and men in support for religious law.

- There is no significant difference in the level of personal piety between the majority who condemn terrorism and the fringe minority who condone it.

- Those who condone terrorism admire Western freedom and liberty as much as the moderate majority.

Gallup would pose research questions to the dataset and eagerly dig for the answers. For example, how do young people's views of the West differ from their elders' views? (Answer: Not much.) Who most values democracy in the Muslim world?

(Answer: Diverse group who are more educated and more religious than those who do not.) Researchers looked at demographic differences within a country, between countries, and among predominantly Muslim and Western nations.

They looked at point-of-view breakouts, such as: How are those who condemn the events of 9/11 different from the fringe minority who condone them? They also used sophisticated statistical techniques to determine key drivers for such things as extremist views. Was it poverty? Illiteracy? Hopelessness? Religious fanaticism? The answer was no on all counts.

An important principle guiding Gallup's analysis was to watch out for "false ahas." As scientists, the researchers knew the importance of always comparing their findings to a "control group" to see if they were indeed a significant characteristic of the Muslim world or a sentiment that transcended culture and religion. Also, how do they really know what is "high" or "low" if they have nothing to compare to? For the purpose of comparison, they often used the American population. For example, they asked residents of predominantly Muslim countries about the moral justifiability of attacks on civilians, and they posed the same question to a representative sample of Americans. What did they find? Levels of support for this common definition of terrorism were no higher in Muslim lands than they were among the general American population, and with few exceptions, did not exceed percentages in the single digits.

Gallup then attempted to piece together the numbers into a coherent story — a potential explanation for the existing data. It is important to note that Gallup developed the ideas of this book by making deductions directly from the data. The company did not begin this research with a theory to test or prove. Rather, it sought to build answers to important questions from the ground up, derived directly from the evidence.

Gallup came to think of each finding as uncovering a pixel in a huge photograph. With each question researchers posed to the data, they discovered a new shade, a new point of color, little by little, until they stood back and saw a clear picture emerge.

Phase 5: Analysis to Aha!: Cultural Context

Once a coherent framework was built through deep analysis of the data, it was time to dress this skeleton in cultural context. This phase — led by Professor John L. Esposito, co-author of this book and one of the leading experts in the field of Islamic studies, and Dalia Mogahed, co-author of this book and executive director of the Gallup Center for Muslim Studies — combined years of scholarship and field experience to give the analysis cultural relevance. Why was the analysis important or surprising? What may have led up to this situation between the Muslim world and the West, and what is at the heart of it? What supporting evidence can other studies offer? How can Gallup make sense of this analysis in the wider cultural context of the Muslim world? These were the questions that this phase of the work answered. The results of this process are the discoveries and insights shared in this book.

Notes

Introduction: Islam's Silenced Majority

[1] Office of the Press Secretary. (2001, September 20). *Address to a joint session of Congress and the American people*. Retrieved September 14, 2007, from http://www.whitehouse.gov/news/releases/2001/09/20010920-8.html

[2] Saad, L. (2006, August 10). Anti-Muslim sentiments fairly commonplace. *Gallup Poll News Service*. Retrieved December 27, 2007, from http://www.gallup.com/poll/24073/AntiMuslim-Sentiments-Fairly-Commonplace.aspx

[3] Mogahed, D., & Newport, F. (2007, February 2). Americans: people in Muslim countries have negative views of U.S. *Gallup Poll News Service*. Retrieved December 27, 2007, from http://www.gallup.com/poll/26350/Americans-People-Muslim-Countries-Negative-Views-US.aspx

Chapter 1: Who Are Muslims?

[4] Mogahed, D. (2006, February 8). Americans' views of the Islamic world. *Gallup Poll News Service*. Retrieved December 27, 2007, from http://www.gallup.com/poll/21349/Americans-Views-Islamic-World.aspx

[5] Organization of the Islamic Conference. Member states information. Retrieved September 14, 2007, from http://www.oic-oci.org/

[6] Gallup Poll, based on telephone interviews with 808 national adults, aged 18 and older, conducted February 17-22, 2006. Respondents were randomly drawn from Gallup's household panel, which was originally recruited through random selection methods. For results based on this sample, one can say with 95% confidence that the margin of sampling error is ±4 percentage points.

[7] Burkholder, R. (2002, September 17). The role of prayer in Islamic world. *Gallup Poll News Service*. Retrieved December 27, 2007, from http://www.gallup.com/poll/6814/Role-Prayer-Islamic-World.aspx

[8] Malcolm X, Jeddah, Saudi Arabia, April 20, 1964, *Malcolm X speaks: selected speeches and statements*, ed. George Breitman (New York: Grove Press, 1990), p. 59.

[9] Esposito, J.L. (2002). *What everyone needs to know about Islam*. New York: Oxford University Press.

[10] Esposito, J.L. Jihad: holy or unholy war? Retrieved September 14, 2007, from the Alliance of Civilizations Web site: http://www.unaoc.org/repository/Esposito_Jihad_Holy_Unholy.pdf

Chapter 2: Democracy or Theocracy?

[11] Fukuyama, F. (2001, October 11). The West has won. *The Guardian*. Retrieved September 14, 2007, from http://www.guardian.co.uk/waronterror/story/0,,567333,00.html

[12] 10 Downing Street. (2003, March 20). *Prime Minister's address to the nation*. Retrieved September 14, 2007, from http://www.pm.gov.uk/output/Page3327.asp

[13] Jordan: year in brief 2005 – a chronology of democratic developments. (2006, January 15). *IRIN*. Retrieved September 14, 2007, from http://www.irinnews.info/S_report.asp?ReportID=51118&Select Region=Middle_East

[14] Samaan, M. (2006, December 29). Opposition fear constitutional amendments would lead to political setback. *Daily News Egypt*. Retrieved September 14, 2007, from http://www.dailystaregypt.com/ article.aspx?ArticleID=4724

[15] Fattah, H. (2007, April 25). Momentum for democratic reform wanes in Saudi Arabia. *International Herald Tribune*. Retrieved September 14, 2007, from http://www.iht.com/articles/2007/04/25/europe/saudi.php

[16] Shadid, A. (2007, January 22). War's Arab supporters bitter over its results. *The Washington Post*. Retrieved September 14, 2007, from http://www.washingtonpost.com/wp-dyn/content/article/2007/01/21/ AR2007012101282.html

[17] Dinmore, G. (2007, January 17). A uniform trend? How democracy worldwide is on the back foot. *The Financial Times*. Retrieved September 14, 2007, from http://www.ft.com/cms/s/0/5bb0e9a2-a5d0-11db-a4e0-0000779e2340.html

[18] Shadid, A. (2007, January 22). War's Arab supporters bitter over its results. *The Washington Post*. Retrieved September 14, 2007, from http://www.washingtonpost.com/wp-dyn/content/article/2007/01/21/ AR2007012101282.html

[19] Syrian Press Highlights. (2007, January 29). *BBC Worldwide Monitoring*. Retrieved September 14, 2007, from LexisNexis.

[20] Ibid.

[21] *aljazeera* magazine is not related to the Arabic satellite TV channel, Al Jazeera, which operates Web sites in both Arabic (www.aljazeera.net) and English (english.aljazeera.net) or *Al-Jazeera* newspaper of Saudi Arabia.

[22] *aljazeera* magazine. Let's talk. Irretrievable as of September 14, 2007, from http://www.aljazeera.com/cgi-bin/news_service/article_full_story.asp?service_id=12799

[23] Tribune News Services (2000, June 20). A 4th state in Nigeria proclaims Islamic law. *Chicago Tribune*, p. 10.

[24] Gyasi, I.K. (2006, April 10). The shame of Islam today. *Ghanaian Chronicle*. Retrieved September 14, 2007, from LexisNexis.

[25] Pitman, T. (2003, September 26). Stoning death sentence overruled. *The Toronto Star*, p. A14.

[26] Lippman, M., McConville, S., & Yerushalmi, M. (1988). *Islamic criminal law and procedure: an introduction*. New York: Praeger Publishers.

[27] Mishal, S. (1978). *West Bank/East Bank: the Palestinians in Jordan, 1949-1967*. New Haven and London: Yale University Press.

[28] Risen, J. (2000). Secrets of history: the CIA in Iran. *New York Times Special Report*. Retrieved September 14, 2007, from http://www.nytimes.com/library/world/mideast/041600iran-cia-index.html

[29] Lerner, D. (1958). *The passing of traditional society: modernizing the Middle East*. Glencoe, Illinois: Free Press.

[30] Kenyan student, interview with Hadia Mubarak, Fatah University, Istanbul, Turkey, February 27, 2006.

[31] Murphy, D. (2003, September 16). Who's radicalizing Indonesia's schools? *The Christian Science Monitor*. Retrieved September 14, 2007, from http://www.csmonitor.com/2003/0916/p07s01-woap.html

[32] Ibid.

[33] Kenyan student, interview with Hadia Mubarak, Fatah University, Istanbul, Turkey, February 27, 2006.

[34] Agencies. (2006, January 20). Shiite parties win Iraq poll. *Gulf News*. Retrieved September 14, 2007, from http://archive.gulfnews.com/indepth/iraqelection/sub_story/10013187.html

[35] *The Economist* (2002, November). Erodgan triumphs – with plenty of help from his enemies. *The Economist*. Retrieved September 14, 2007, from http://www.economist.com/background/displaystory.cfm?story_id=1433284

[36] Ghattas, K. (2005, April 23). Conservatives 'win' Saudi polls. *BBC News*. Retrieved September 14, 2007, from http://news.bbc.co.uk/2/middle_east/44477315.stm

[37] *The Economist* (2006, April 20). Broken promises. *The Economist*. Retrieved September 14, 2007, from http://www.economist.com/opinion/displaystory.cfm?story_id=6831997

[38] Deane, C., & Frears, D. (2006, March 9). Negative perception of Islam rising. *The Washington Post*. Retrieved September 14, 2007, from http://www.washingtonpost.com/wp-dyn/content/article/2006/03/08/AR2006030802221_pf.html

[39] Pew Research Center for the People & the Press and the Pew Forum on Religion & Public Life. Results for this survey are based on telephone interviews conducted under the direction of Princeton Survey Research Associates International among a nationwide sample of 2,000 adults, 18 years of age or older, from July 7-17, 2005. For results based on the total sample, one can say with 95% confidence that the error attributable to sampling is ±2.5 percentage points. For results based on Form 1 (N=1,000) or Form 2 (N=1,000) only, the error attributable to sampling is ±3.5 percentage points.

[40] Burkina Faso, Nigeria, Sierra Leone, Tajikistan, Chad, Kazakhstan, Tanzania, and Turkey were the exceptions.

[41] Gallup Poll, based on telephone interviews with 808 national adults, aged 18 and older, conducted February 17-22, 2006. Respondents were randomly drawn from Gallup's household panel, which was originally recruited through random selection methods. For results based on this sample, one can say with 95% confidence that the margin of sampling error is ±4 percentage points.

[42] Carroll, R. (2005, August 15). Women battle for rights in new Iraq. *The Guardian*. Retrieved September 14, 2007, from http://www.guardian.co.uk/gender/story/0,,1549354,00.html

[43] Krane, J. (2004, February 16). U.S. administrator threatens veto of Iraqi Islamic law measure. The Associated Press. Retrieved September 14, 2007, from LexisNexis.

[44] *BBC News*. (2003, April 25). Rumsfeld rejects 'cleric-led' rule. *BBC News*. Retrieved September 14, 2007, from http://news.bbc.co.uk/1/hi/world/middle_east/2975333.stm

[45] Carroll, J. (2005, February 25). Iraqi women eye Islamic law. *The Christian Science Monitor*. Retrieved September 14, 2007, from http://www.csmonitor.com/2005/0225/p07s02-woiq.html

[46] Sisters in Islam. (2003, March 16). Campaign for monogamy; by the Coalition on Women's Rights in Islam. Retrieved September 14, 2007, from http://www.sistersinislam.org.my/pressstatement/16032003.htm

[47] Esposito, J.L., & Voll, J. (2001, November/December). Islam and democracy. *Humanities*. Retrieved September 14, 2007, from http://www.neh.gov/news/humanities/2001-11/islam.html

[48] Esposito, J.L. (2003, April/May). Practice and theory. *Boston Review*. Retrieved September 14, 2007, from http://bostonreview.net/BR28.2/esposito.html

[49] Decherf, D. (2001, July). French views of religious freedom. *U.S.-France Analysis*. Retrieved September 14, 2007, from http://www.brookings.edu/fp/cuse/analysis/relfreedom.htm

[50] Ahmad, K. (1976). *Islam: principles and characteristics* in Kurshid Ahmad, ed., *Islam: Its meaning and message*. London: Islamic Council of Europe, p. 43.

[51] Afghanistan, Indonesia, Lebanon, Malaysia, Senegal, Sierra Leone, Burkina Faso, Nigeria, Niger, and Tanzania.

[52] U.S. State Department. (2002, December 4). *Towards greater democracy in the Muslim world*. Retrieved September 14, 2007, from http://www.state.gov/s/p/rem/15686.htm

[53] Dinmore, G. (2007, January 17). A uniform trend? How democracy worldwide is on the back foot. *The Financial Times*. Retrieved September 14, 2007, from http://www.ft.com/cms/s/0/5bb0e9a2-a5d0-11db-a4e0-0000779e2340.html

[54] Shadid, A. (2007, January 22). War's Arab supporters bitter over its results. *The Washington Post*. Retrieved September 14, 2007, from http://www.washingtonpost.com/wp-dyn/content/article/2007/01/21/AR2007012101282.html

[55] To complete the analysis, we chose the 10 most populous majority Muslim countries, which make up 80% of the global Muslim population: Egypt, Indonesia, Jordan, Saudi Arabia, Turkey, Lebanon, Pakistan, Morocco, Iran, and Bangladesh.

Chapter 3: What Makes a Radical?

[56] Robert McNamara. (1996, April 16). *A life in public service: conversation with Robert McNamara*, interview by Harry Kreisler. Berkeley, California: Regents of the University of California. Retrieved September 16, 2007, from http://globetrotter.berkeley.edu/McNamara/mcnamara7.html

[57] *BBC News*. (2006, April 23). West is on a crusade – Bin Laden. *BBC News*. Retrieved September 16, 2007, from http://news.bbc.co.uk/2/hi/middle_east/4936284.stm

[58] Saad Eddin Ibrahim (1982, February). Egypt's Islamic militants. *MERIP Reports* 103. See also Saad Eddin Ibrahim, Islamic militancy as social movement, in Ali E. Hillal Dessouki. ed., *Islamic Resurgence in the Arab World*. New York: Praeger, p.128-31, and Emmanuel Sivan. (1990). *Radical Islam: medieval theology and modern politics*. New Haven: Yale University Press, p. 118-19.

[59] *BBC News.* (2002, July 16). Profile: Omar Saeed Sheikh. *BBC News.* Retrieved September 16, 2007, from http://news.bbc.co.uk/1/hi/uk/1804710.stm

[60] To complete the analysis, we chose the 10 most populous majority Muslim countries, which make up 80% of the global Muslim population: Egypt, Indonesia, Jordan, Saudi Arabia, Turkey, Lebanon, Pakistan, Morocco, Iran, and Bangladesh.

[61] Handwerk, Brian. (2004, December 13). Female suicide bombers: dying to kill. *National Geographic Channel.* Retrieved September 16, 2007, from http://news.nationalgeographic.com/news/2004/12/1213_041213_tv_suicide_bombers.html

[62] Harris, Sam. (2004, December 2). 'Mired in a religious war.' *Washington Times.*

[63] Auster, Lawrence. (2005, January 28). The search for moderate Islam. *FrontPageMagazine.com.* Retrieved September 16, 2007, from http://www.frontpagemag.com/Articles/Read.aspx?GUID={5F4D7BB5-CA89-4C09-986B-67CF241C2098}

[64] Munro, D. (1895). *Translations and reprints from the original sources of European history, Vol. 1:2.* Philadelphia: University of Pennsylvania. Retrieved September 16, 2007, from http://www.fordham.edu/halsall/source/urban2-5vers.html

[65] From a statement given by Mark Juergensmeyer at the International Summit on Democracy, Terrorism, and Security, March 8-11, 2005, in Madrid, Spain.

[66] Robert Pape. (2005, July 18). *The logic of suicide terrorism*, interview by Scott McConnell. *The American Conservative*. Retrieved September 16, 2007, from http://amconmag.com/2005_07_18/article.html

[67] Pape, Robert. (2005). *Dying to win: the strategic logic of suicide terrorism*. New York: Random House, p. 130.

[68] Ibid.

[69] Gerges, F. (2006, October 13). Stoking Muslim anger. *International Herald Tribune*. Retrieved September 16, 2007, from http://www.iht.com/articles/2006/10/13/opinion/edgerges.php

[70] Bortin, M. (2006, June 29). For Muslims and West, antipathy and mistrust. *International Herald Tribune*. Retrieved September 16, 2007, from http://www.iht.com/articles/2006/06/22/news/pew2.php

[71] Gerges, F. (2006, October 13). Stoking Muslim anger. *International Herald Tribune*. Retrieved September 16, 2007, from http://www.iht.com/articles/2006/10/13/opinion/edgerges.php

[72] Female engineering student, interview with Hadia Mubarak, University of Jordan, Amman, Jordan, March 6, 2006.

[73] These findings are from surveys in Egypt, Morocco, Pakistan, and Indonesia conducted from December 2006 to February 2007 by WorldPublicOpinion.org with support from the START Consortium at the University of Maryland. Retrieved September 16, 2007, from http://www.worldpublicopinion.org/pipa/articles/home_page/346.php?nid=&id=&pnt=346&lb=hmpg1

[74] Shaheen, J. (2001). *Reel bad Arabs: how Hollywood vilifies a people*. New York: Olive Branch Press.

[75] Jordanian high school student, interview with Hadia Mubarak, Amman, Jordan, March 6, 2006.

[76] *BBC News.* (2005, September 2). London bomber video aired on TV. *BBC News.* Retrieved September 16, 2007, from http://news.bbc. co.uk/2/hi/uk_news/4206708.stm

[77] Bulliet, R. (2004). *The case for Islamo-Christian civilization.* New York: Columbia University Press.

[78] WorldPublicOpinion.org Poll. Most questions were asked in a Dec. 6-11 survey with a nationwide sample of 1,004 Americans (margin of error ±3.2-3.8% depending on whether the question was asked to the whole sample or a three-quarters sample). Another survey was conducted Nov. 21-29 with a nationwide sample of 1,326 Americans (margin of error ±2.7-3.9% depending on whether the question was asked to the whole sample or a subsample). Both polls were fielded by Knowledge Networks, using its nationwide panel, which is randomly selected from the entire adult population and subsequently provided Internet access. Retrieved September 18, 2007, from http://www.worldpublicopinion. org/pipa/pdf/jan07/Iran_Jan07_rpt.pdf

[79] Ballen, K. (2007, February 23). The myth of Muslim support for terror. *The Christian Science Monitor.* Retrieved September 18, 2007, from http://www.csmonitor.com/2007/0223/p09s01-coop.html

[80] WorldPublicOpinion.org Poll. Most questions were asked in a Dec. 6-11 survey with a nationwide sample of 1,004 Americans (margin of error ±3.2-3.8% depending on whether the question was asked to the whole sample or a three-quarters sample). Another survey was conducted Nov. 21-29 with a nationwide sample of 1,326 Americans (margin of error ±2.7-3.9% depending on whether the question was asked to the whole sample or a subsample). Both polls were fielded by Knowledge Networks, using its nationwide panel, which is randomly selected from

the entire adult population and subsequently provided Internet access. Retrieved September 18, 2007, from http://www.worldpublicopinion. org/pipa/pdf/jan07/Iran_Jan07_rpt.pdf

[81] Gerges, F. (2006, October 13). Stoking Muslim anger. *International Herald Tribune.* Retrieved September 16, 2007, from http://www.iht. com/articles/2006/10/13/opinion/edgerges.php

Chapter 4: What Do Women Want?

[82] Wafa Sultan. (2006, February 21). Arab-American psychiatrist Wafa Sultan: there is no clash of civilizations but a clash between the mentality of the middle ages and that of the 21st century, television interview on Al-Jazeera TV. Transcript retrieved September 18, 2007, from http://www.memritv.org/clip_transcript/en/1050.htm

[83] Honor killings are an ancient tradition still sometimes observed; a male member of the family kills a female relative for tarnishing the family image.

[84] Office of the First Lady. (2001, November 17). Radio address by Mrs. Bush. Retrieved September 18, 2007, from http://www.whitehouse.gov/ news/releases/2001/11/20011117.html

[85] Van Sommer, A., & Zwemer, S. (1907). *Our Moslem sisters: a cry of need from lands of darkness interpreted by those who heard it.* New York: The Young People's Missionary Movement.

[86] Kamalipour, Y. (1995). *The U.S. media and the Middle East: image and perception.* Westport, Connecticut: Praeger Publishers.

[87] United Nations Development Programme. (2006). Arab human development report 2005: towards the rise of women in the Arab world. New York: United Nations Development Programme.

[88] Souad Saleh. (2005, October 27-November 2). Souad Saleh: Time to tear down divides, interview by Gamal Nkrumah. *Al-Ahram Weekly*. Retrieved September 18, 2007, from http://weekly.ahram.org.eg/2005/766/profile.htm

[89] Jonathan Hayden, personal written statement.

[90] Hirsi Ali, A. (2005, October 29). Muslim women are the key to change. *London Times*. Retrieved September 18, 2007, from http://www.timesonline.co.uk/tol/news/article616428.ece

[91] Lazreg, M. (1994). *The eloquence of silence: Algerian women in question*. London: Routledge, p. 136.

[92] Johnson, B. (2001, September 27). What Islamic terrorists are really afraid of is women. *The Daily Telegraph*. Retrieved September 18, 2007, from http://www.telegraph.co.uk/opinion/main.jhtml?xml=/opinion/2001/09/27/do02.xml

[93] Amin, Q. *"Tahrir al-mar'a." Al-Amal al-kamila li Qasim Amin*, 2 vols., ed. Muhammad 'Amara (Beirut: Al'mu'assasa al-'arabiya lil-dirasat wa'l nashr, 1976), 69-72. See also Leila Ahmed, *Women and Gender in Islam*, 155. See also Lila Abu-Lughod, "The Marriage of Feminism and Islamism in Egypt: Selective Repudiation as a Dynamic of Postcolonial Politics," in *Remaking Women: Feminism and Modernity in the Middle East*, ed. Abu-Lughod (Princeton, NJ: Princeton University Press, 1998), 256.

[94] Bullock, K. (2004, February-March). Hijab and contemporary Muslim women. *The Message International*. Retrieved September 18, 2007, from http://www.messageonline.org/2004febmarch/cover1_opt.pdf

[95] American University. Unpublished survey. "Islamic in the Age of Globalization" Project.

[96] Pew Global Attitudes Project. (2006). The great divide: how Westerners and Muslims view each other. Retrieved September 18, 2007, from http://pewglobal.org/reports/display.php?ReportID=253

[97] Written statement by Frankie Martin, reproduced with permission.

[98] Interviewing was conducted by Gallup during the period of March 22 through April 9, 2004.

[99] Mahmood, S. (2005). *Politics of piety: the Islamic revival and the feminist subject*. Princeton, New Jersey: Princeton University Press, p. 44-45.

[100] Ibid.

[101] Ahsan, S. (2006, September 2). Chorus gets louder: resentment grows against plan to shift women praying area in Grand Mosque. *The Saudi Gazette*. Retrieved September 18, 2007, from http://www.saudigazette. com.sa/index.php?option=com_content&task=view&id=14445& Itemid=116

[102] *Al-Iqtissadiya*. (2006, August 29). Arabic language newspaper.

[103] Al-Fassi, H. (2006, August 30). The rights of women in the Grand Mosque. *Arab News*. Retrieved September 17, 2007, from http://www. arabnews.com/?page=7&section=0&article=78202&d=30&m=8&y= 2006.

[104] Ibid.

[105] Al-Jazeera & Reuters. (2006, September 15). Women face curbs in Makka mosque. *Al-Jazeera.net*. Retrieved September 18, 2007, from http://english.aljazeera.net/English/Archive/ Archive?ArchiveID=35489

[106] Quraishi, A. (1997). Her honor: an Islamic critique of the rape laws of Pakistan from a woman-sensitive perspective. *Michigan Journal of International Law, Vol. 18.* Retrieved September 18, 2007, from http://law.wisc.edu/faculty/download.php?iID=175

[107] Hassan, F. (2006, November 28). Women's protection bill: perception and realities. *Islamonline.* Retrieved September 18, 2007, from http://www.islamonline.net/servlet/Satellite?c=Article_C&cid=116454589795 3&pagename=Zone-English-Living_Shariah/LSELayout

[108] United Nations Children's Fund. (2005). Female genital mutilation/cutting: a statistical exploration. United Nations Children's Fund. Retrieved September 18, 2007, from http://www.unicef.org/publications/files/FGM-C_final_10_October.pdf

[109] El Ahl, A. (2006, December 6). Theologians battle female circumcision. *Spiegel.* Retrieved September 18, 2007, from http://www.spiegel.de/international/spiegel/0,1518,452790,00.html

[110] Ottaway, M. (2004, July). Avoiding the women's rights trap. *Arab Reform Bulletin.* Retrieved September 18, 2007, from http://www.carnegieendowment.org/publications/index.cfm?fa=view&id=1590

[111] Mahmood, S. (2005). *Politics of piety: the Islamic revival and the feminist subject.* Princeton, New Jersey: Princeton University Press, p. 44.

[112] Iran, Pakistan, Lebanon, Morocco, Saudi Arabia, Egypt, Jordan, Turkey.

[113] Lamis Al-Nasser, Bashir al-Bilbisi, and Diana 'Atiyyat, *Al-'Unf did al-mar'a fil-mujtama' al-urduni: Al-khasa'is al-dimoghrafiyya lil-dahaya wal-junat* (Amman: Al-Mutlaqa al-Insni li Huqu al-Mar'a, 1998), 14.

[114] Sonbol, A. (2003). *Women of Jordan: Islam, labor, and the law.* Syracuse, New York: Syracuse University Press, p. 191-192.

[115] Dinmore, G. (2005, September 27). Saudi students rebuff US communications guru. *Financial Times.* Retrieved September 18, 2007, from http://www.ft.com/cms/s/0/ebe0f15c-2fa2-11da-8b51-00000e2511c8.html

[116] Ibid.

[117] Egypt, Iran, Iraq, Jordan, Kuwait, Lebanon, Morocco, Nigeria, Pakistan, Palestine, Saudi Arabia, Senegal, Turkey, Tanzania, and United Arab Emirates.

[118] Hibri, A. (2004). Who defines women's rights? A third world woman's response. *Human Rights Brief.* Retrieved September 18, 2007, from http://www.wcl.american.edu/hrbrief/v2i1/alhibr21.htm

[119] Inglehart, R., & Welzel, C. (2005). *Modernization, culture change and democracy: the human development sequence.* New York: Cambridge University Press.

[120] United Nations Development Programme. (2006). Arab human development report 2005: towards the rise of women in the Arab world. New York: United Nations Development Programme.

[121] Lughod, L. (2003). Saving Muslim women or standing with them?: on images, ethics, and war in our times. *Insaniyaat.* Retrieved September 18, 2007, from http://www.aucegypt.edu/academic/insanyat/Issue%20I/I-article1.htm

[122] Dedrick, A. (2006, May 26). Feminism can't solve all, Muslim speaker advises. *The Stanford Daily*. Retrieved September 18, 2007, from http://daily.stanford.edu/article/2006/5/26/ feminismCantSolveAllMuslimSpeakerAdvises

[123] Ibid.

[124] Teves, O. (2003, November 7). Miss Afghanistan conflicted about bikini. The Associated Press. Retrieved September 18, 2007, from LexisNexis.

Chapter 5: Clash or Coexistence?

[125] Krastev, N. (2004, December 10). World: UN forum explores ways to fight 'Islamophobia'. *Radio Free Europe*. Retrieved September 18, 2007, from http://www.rferl.org/featuresarticle/2004/12/7e9a94b2-7e8d-4811-a017-1500bde65e62.html

[126] The Jewish Population of the World (2006). Jewish Virtual Library. Retrieved September 18, 2007, from http://www.jewishvirtuallibrary.org/jsource/Judaism/jewpop.html

[127] Esposito, J.L. (2006, November 6). Islamophobia. Prince Alwaleed Bin Talal Center for Muslim-Christian Understanding. Retrieved September 18, 2007, from http://blogs.georgetown.edu/?id=20320

[128] Council on Foreign Relations. (2005, September 22). Evangelicals and the Middle East. Council on Foreign Relations. Retrieved September 18, 2007, from http://www.cfr.org/publication/8911/ evangelicals_and_the_middle_east_rush_transcript_federal_news_ service_inc.html?breadcrumb=%2Fbios%2F5850%2Fnancy_e_roman

[129] Pipes, D. (2002, October 25). Beltway snipers: converts to violence? *New York Post*. Retrieved September 18, 2007, from http://www. danielpipes.org/article/492

[130] Caldwell, C. (2004, October 4). Islamic Europe? *The Weekly Standard*. Retrieved September 18, 2007, from http://www.weeklystandard.com/ Utilities/printer_preview.asp?idArticle=4685&R=C7B15

[131] Primor, A. (2002, April). Le Pen ultimate. *Haaretz*. Retrieved September 18, 2007, from http://news.haaretz.co.il/hasen/pages/ShArt. jhtml?itemNo=153419

[132] Pettersson, C. (2004, July 19). Right-wing politicians want to ban Islam. *Nettavisen*. Retrieved September 18, 2007, from http://pub.tv2. no/nettavisen/english/article254421.ece

[133] Allen, C., & Nielsen, J. (2002, May). Summary report on Islamophobia in the EU after 11 September 2001. European Monitoring Centre on Racism and Xenophobia. Retrieved September 18, 2007, from http://fra.europa.eu/fra/material/pub/anti-islam/Synthesis-report_en.pdf

[134] Husain, S. (2006, February 20). Danish firm loses $1.5m per day. *Gulf News*. Retrieved September 18, 2007, from http://archive.gulf-news.com/indepth/danishcontroversy/more_stories/10020109.html

[135] Barzak, I. (2006, February 2). Protests over Prophet Muhammad cartoons escalate in Islamic world. The Associated Press. Retrieved September 18, 2007, from LexisNexis.

[136] Landsberg, M., & Reitman, V. (2005, August 11). Watts riots: 40 years later. *The Los Angeles Times*. Retrieved September 18, 2007, from http://www.latimes.com/news/local/la-me-watts11aug11,0,7619426. story?coll=la-home-headlines

[137] Williamson, S. (2006). Five ways to compute the relative value of a U.S. dollar amount, 1790-2005. *MeasuringWorth.com*. Retrieved September 18, 2007, from http://www.measuringworth.com/calculators/compare/

[138] Moore, D. (2006, February 14). Public critical of European newspapers showing Mohammed cartoon. *Gallup News Service*. Retrieved December 27, 2007, from http://www.gallup.com/poll/21427/Public-Critical-European-Newspapers-Showing-Mohammed-Cartoon.aspx

[139] *BBC News*. (2003, December 23). Should Islamic headscarves be banned in schools? *BBC News*. Retrieved September 18, 2007, from http://news.bbc.co.uk/1/hi/talking_point/3343437.stm

[140] Libreria Editrice Vaticana. (2006, September 12). Meeting with the representatives of science: lecture of the holy father. Retrieved September 18, 2007, from http://www.vatican.va/holy_father/benedict_xvi/speeches/2006/september/documents/hf_ben-xvi_spe_20060912_university-regensburg_en.html

[141] Open Letter to Pope Benedict XVI. (2006). *Islamica Magazine*. Retrieved September 18, 2007, from http://www.islamicamagazine.com/issue18/openletter18_lowres.pdf

[142] Mogahed, D., & Newport, F. (2007, February 2). Americans: people in Muslim countries have negative views of U.S. *Gallup News Service*. Retrieved December 27, 2007, from http://www.gallup.com/poll/26350/Americans-People-Muslim-Countries-Negative-Views-US.aspx

[143] Saad, L. (2006, August 10). Anti-Muslim sentiments fairly commonplace. *Gallup News Service*. Retrieved December 27, 2007, from http://www.gallup.com/poll/24073/AntiMuslim-Sentiments-Fairly-Commonplace.aspx

[144] Gallup Poll Editors. (2002). The 2002 Gallup Poll of the Islamic World: subscriber report. Princeton, New Jersey: Gallup, Inc.

[145] Pew Global Attitudes Project (2002). Islamic extremism: common concern for Muslim and Western publics. Retrieved September 18, 2007, from http://pewglobal.org/reports/display.php?ReportID=248

[146] Gallup Poll. Results are based on telephone interviews with 2,388 national adults, aged 18 and older, conducted June 4-24, 2007, including oversamples of blacks and Hispanics that are weighted to reflect their proportions in the general population. For results based on the total sample of national adults, one can say with 95% confidence that the maximum margin of sampling error is ±5 percentage points.

Gallup Press exists to educate and inform the people who govern, manage, teach, and lead the world's six billion citizens. Each book meets Gallup's requirements of integrity, trust, and independence and is based on a Gallup-approved science and research.